D0571716

Freedom Betrayed

Freedom Betrayed

How America Led a Global Democratic Revolution, Won the Cold War, and Walked Away

Michael A. Ledeen

The AEI Press

Publisher for the American Enterprise Institute

WASHINGTON, D.C.

1996

Available in the United States from the AEI Press, c/o Publisher Resources Inc., 1224 Heil Quaker Blvd., P.O. Box 7001, La Vergne, TN 37086-7001. Distributed outside the United States by arrangement with Eurospan, 3 Henrietta Street, London WC2E 8LU England.

Library of Congress Cataloging-in-Publication Data

Ledeen, Michael Arthur, 1941–.
    Freedom betrayed : how America led a global democratic revolution, won the cold war, and walked away / Michael A. Ledeen.
    p. cm.
    Includes bibliographical references and index.
    ISBN 0-8447-3992-8 (alk. paper)
    1. United States—Foreign relations—1989– 2. United States—Politics and government—1989– 3. World Politics—1985–1995.
4. Democracy—History—20th century. 5. Cold War. I. Title.
    E840.L4 1996
    324.73—dc20   96-29292
                                        CIP

THE AEI PRESS
Publisher for the American Enterprise Institute
1150 17th Street, N.W., Washington, D.C. 20036

Printed in the United States of America

CONTENTS

ACKNOWLEDGMENTS

Many of the themes here have been developed over the years in essays in the *American Spectator,* and I owe a great debt to Bob Tyrrell and Wlady Plesczynski for giving me space to publish them, and many helpful suggestions that improved them. The material on Japan appeared in a somewhat different context in the *Washingtonian*, and thanks to Jack Limpert and Phillip Merrill for permission to reprint it in this form. Other material was first published in Op-Ed articles in the *Wall Street Journal,* and my thanks to the editors for permission to use it here. Thanks also to Bill Kristol and Fred Barnes, for permission to use material that first appeared in the *Weekly Standard.*

Nowadays, scholarly work by those of us outside the academy depends on financial and intellectual support from special people and special places. I have had the good fortune to work at one of the very best places, the American Enterprise Institute. My thanks to Chris DeMuth, its president, Vice President David Gerson, and my colleagues at AEI, for their encouragement and trenchant criticism. Dana Lane was an excellent editor.

My work at AEI has been supported over the years by the Smith Richardson Foundation and the Sarah Scaife Foundation, as well as by dozens of individuals and companies that have generously endowed the Freedom Chair. I hope they will take pleasure in this result of their philanthropy. Thanks also to Michael Milken, who has given me the chance to work with him and his fine team at the Milken Institute for Job and Capital Formation.

Special thanks are due to Barbara Ledeen, who believed in the value of this book long after I had serious doubts. Such a wife, who brightens all my days and challenges me to keep tackling the hardest problems with the same rigor she brings to her own work, is a rare blessing.

If I have accurately described the nature of the Soviet Empire and its collapse, much of the credit must go to Vladimir Bukovsky, who truly fulfilled Marx's entreaty by both understanding the Soviet world and changing it. On the crucial issue of East-West technology transfer, I have been fortunate to have had the opportunity to learn firsthand from Stephen Bryen, the foremost authority on the subject. I am also grateful to Herb Meyer, Walter Dean Burnham, Giuliano Ferrara, Lucio Colletti, and Rosario Romeo for many years of animated discussion. None of them will be in full agreement with this book, and some of them will be in substantial disagreement with much of it, but all have helped me think it through.

The basic argument of *Freedom Betrayed*—that one cannot understand contemporary events by trying to analyze the separate pieces one by one but only in a broader historical context—no doubt stems from my training as a historian and has been reinforced by years of work with three of the outstanding scholars of our time: Walter Laqueur, George L. Mosse, and Renzo De Felice. My deepest thanks to all of them.

Renzo De Felice's courageous fight against those who tried to use the history of fascism as a political weapon is described in the pages that follow. His untimely death in May 1996 deprives us of a tireless seeker of the truth and an exceptional teacher. *Freedom Betrayed,* much of which was debated in his living room in Rome, is dedicated to his memory.

Freedom Betrayed

1

❖

INTRODUCTION

This is the Age of the Second Democratic Revolution. Inspired by the values of the American Revolution, supported and advanced by American military power and a remarkable generation of democratic leaders, the revolution has swept the world. Antidemocratic regimes have fallen in Europe, Asia, Latin America, and Africa. Parliaments from the Italian Chamber of Deputies to the American Congress have been radically transformed. The cult of the state—the belief that government is better suited than individuals or spontaneous, temporary organizations to solve mankind's basic problems—came under global assault, and in a surprising number of countries the powers of once-oppressive central governments were greatly reduced. Tyranny has been routed on every continent, and hopeful democrats, many of them survivors of frightful repression, torture, and mass murder, have proclaimed the people's right to choose their own government and live under a system of law rather than arbitrary *diktat*. When the Soviet Empire collapsed at the beginning of this decade, it seemed that we might soon see democracy everywhere triumphant and that our children could live in a world governed by our highest ideals.

Yet just at the moment our values had swept the world, our leaders betrayed the Democratic Revolution, abandoned our historic mission, and stood by as the forces of tyranny reestablished much of their evil sway. The enemies of democracy—seemingly

1

overthrown just a few years ago—are becoming stronger in much of the former Soviet Empire, and in some cases the very same men and women who inflicted the Communist terror are now returning to power, wrapped in a newfound mantle of democratic respectability. Having won the cold war, we are in danger of seeing our historic victory overwhelmed by a new generation of tyrants.

This is not new for the United States: twice before in this century we led a successful campaign against the enemies of democracy but tragically bungled the peace. We have only an occasional international vocation, and our history attests to our reluctance to play the Great Game. German U-boats torpedoed us into World War I, Japanese Zeroes bombed us into World War II, and Stalin's voracious appetite for power roused us from our postwar slumbers in the late 1940s. Left to our own devices, we would have waited longer, possibly beyond the moment of survival. An American sage once remarked that "God protects the blind, the drunk, and the United States of America," but one is entitled to suspect that divine benevolence may have its limits. Unfortunately, we have failed to accept that we are condemned to lead the forces of democracy, and, believing that peace is the normal condition of mankind despite millennia of evidence to the contrary, we disarm after each victory. In a typically American triumph of hope over experience, we convince ourselves that this time the others will leave us alone.

Our First Father told us to avoid foreign entanglements, and we cherish his words. Woe to those who tear us from our domestic pursuits and drag us into the gutter of filth and corruption outside our gates! We do not wish to be a part of that world. We do not know its geography, we do not speak its languages, and we do not study its history or its cultures or even its geography. We remember that our ancestors ran from it, and deep in our viscera the antibodies still multiply, to protect us against its poisons. We often forget that we have survived this righteous antipathy because of the blessings of global geography and regional history.

Other peoples might well wish to share our disdain for the "others," but they cannot, for danger lies just across their borders. They have Libyans or Syrians, Hutus or Zulus, Serbs or Mongols; we have Mexicans and Canadians—neighbors, not threatening presences. Others' dreams are drenched with fears of rape, massacre, torture, and death; we worry that our neighbors' labor costs are too low or that their smokestacks lack proper filters.

America's Revolutionary Values

Yet, in our schizophrenic way, even as we separate ourselves from the others, we preach to them our revolutionary values. This, too, is part of our genetic makeup, for even if our leaders remain silent, the radical facts of our existence shake the foundations of the undemocratic and the repressive. That we were frequently unworthy to stand on the pedestal to which we were elevated is beside the point. We drive the revolution because of what we represent: the most successful experiment in human freedom. The boiling blood of Paine and Jefferson is as much a part of our national body and soul as the isolationist warnings of Washington. We do not wish to be part of the outside world, but we do wish to change it, to democratize it, to make it more like us. We are an ideological nation, and our most successful leaders are ideologues. They are seized by what George Bush called the "vision thing," and a good thing it is, for, as we are told in the wisdom of Proverbs, "Where there is no vision, the people perish."

The Second Democratic Revolution is much more than the defeat of communism: it is a worldwide mass movement against all forms of tyranny. One of the themes of this book is that the end of communism was just one moment—albeit the most important—in a global revolution inspired by our values and led by a generation of remarkable leaders from the king of Spain and the British prime minister to the Catholic pope, the leader of a Polish trade union, and the president of the United States. This worldwide revolution began in Spain and Portugal in the mid-1970s and swept Latin America during the Reagan years, as it surged into Eastern and Central Europe, and finally to the Soviet Empire. Today it has come full circle, back to America, as demonstrated by the elections of 1994.

Marx said that the point was not to understand the world, but to change it; yet his own misunderstandings led to catastrophic change. Similar—and in some cases the very same—misunderstandings now threaten our ability to fulfill the promise of this revolutionary moment. Those who opposed the fight against the Soviet Empire are trying to rewrite the history of the struggle between freedom and tyranny, downplaying, and in some cases even denying, the all-important role of the West and, above all, of the United States. The fall of the Soviet Empire is attributed primarily, if not solely, to the failures and errors of the leaders of the Soviet Union, to the vision and courage of Mikhail Gorbachev, and to the leaders of the local democratic movements like Lech Walesa, Andrei Sakharov, and Vaclav Havel. In some cases, it is even argued that the Soviet Empire would have fallen earlier, if only Western leaders—notably Ronald Reagan—had not been so aggressive and combative.

Those who argue this way usually offer a narrow, economic explanation for the fall of the Soviet Empire and the end of communism: the economic system failed, and the empire collapsed accordingly. Yet this is not an explanation at all, for the Soviet system was a failure from the beginning. It did not suddenly come to grief in the 1980s; it was a failure *always*. Russia was the world's greatest grain exporter at the beginning of the twentieth century; it was the world's greatest grain importer by century's end. This decline was not accomplished overnight in the 1980s; the misery of the Russian people was the *leitmotif* of the Communist era. If economic conditions caused the fall of the Soviet Empire, it should have fallen much earlier.

Economic misery cannot explain the twenty years of the Democratic Revolution. Many of the fallen tyrannies were certainly not victims of economic crisis: Pinochet was voted out of office in Chile during an economic boom; the Spanish transition to democracy was achieved during a relatively tranquil economic phase; Corazon Aquino's battle cry was directed against corruption in Manila, not misery; and the Velvet Revolution in Czechoslovakia was not kicked off by bread riots. The failed uprising against Chinese communism was a protest against political oppression, not economic misery. On the other side of the coin, the much-vaunted correlation between wealth and democracy is considerably overstated. Throughout the Middle East, the richest oil-producing countries are tyrannical, despite the growth of a substantial and quite wealthy middle class, while Israel, long one of the poorest, is far and away the most democratic country in the region. The U.S. Democratic Party was decimated in the 1994 elections, even though the economy was very strong, contrary to the conventional wisdom that "Americans vote their pocketbooks." The Democratic Revolution, like most others, was the result of political failure at the top and of superior democratic leadership from below.

The Left's Claim to Revolutionary Tradition

Of all the myths that cloud our understanding, and therefore paralyze our will and action, the most pernicious is that only the Left
has a legitimate claim to the "revolutionary" tradition. According
to this propaganda, anything on the Right is counterrevolutionary, and therefore bad, because contrary to the direction of history. This myth has a distinguished ancestry, dating from the French
Revolution, and in our times it was assiduously promulgated by
the Soviets and their friends in the Western intelligentsia. It retains
astonishing strength even today, although its popularity makes it
impossible to understand the revolution of our time, in which
Ronald Reagan, Margaret Thatcher, Pope John Paul II, and others
led a worldwide revolution directed in large part against the Communist Left.

No particularly deep thinking is required to understand the
revolutionary nature of the policies of those leaders: we have only
to compare the world at the end of Reagan's tenure with the one
he inherited from the unfortunate Jimmy Carter. Carter left us fright-
ened at the expansion of Soviet power and the humiliation of
America, from Iran to Nicaragua; Reagan left us to grapple with
the defeat and collapse of communism. At the end of the Carter
years, we debated whether democratic capitalism could (or even
should) survive; by the end of the 1980s almost everyone acknowledged that both political freedom and a free market are necessary
for intellectual, economic, and political prosperity.

These facts are incompatible with the myth that Reagan was
an ignorant reactionary who jeopardized world peace; yet even
Reagan's appointed heirs eagerly denied that his policies were important or should be continued. Bush and Baker seem not to have
understood that the Soviet Empire fell because its failures were
decisively exploited by the West (led by the United States), because
its values and efforts to expand were challenged—spiritually, militarily, and economically—and because the Soviet leaders, for the
first time since the Bolshevik Revolution, lost confidence in themselves and in the destiny of communism. The empire fell when
Gorbachev and his colleagues had a failure of nerve, while Reagan,
Thatcher, John Paul II, and other Western leaders reinvigorated

the resolve of the West. Had the United States pursued a more courageous foreign policy in the 1970s, challenging the legitimacy of communism instead of elevating the Soviet dictator to equal status with the American president and providing the Kremlin with money and technology the Russians could never have developed by themselves, the empire might well have fallen then and there. Instead, it took another generation to bring the cold war to a successful conclusion. That Bush first and Clinton later conditioned so much of their foreign policy on helping the man in the Kremlin shows an unfortunate confusion about the actual state of world affairs.

Our obligations did not end when the Soviets were beaten; we were obliged to help the newly freed nations face the basic questions: how to build democracy? how to build a free market economy? These are enormously difficult tasks, not least because the damage done by communism was much more profound than had been generally understood. It is not merely the oppression and the day-to-day misery but the violent separation of those peoples from the knowledge, the culture, and the skills of the civilized world, in addition to the violence done to the human spirit by decades of institutionalized terror, that will constitute the lasting legacy of the Bolshevik tyranny. The citizens of the old empire must learn the rules of a free society and the habits of mind of free peoples.[1] The problem is so grave that although most of the world recognizes that democratic capitalism is the best available system, many societies are overwhelmed by the task of achieving it, thereby opening the door for old or new tyrants.

The Democratic Imperative

We Americans have an enormous stake in seeing that the new democracies succeed. If they fail, the blow to the future of democracy—and therefore to our long-term national security—will be monumental. In the short term, our failure will encourage new tyrants, who will inevitably challenge us. Years hence, we will see a generation of embittered democrats come to power, convinced that the United States is not only an unreliable ally but a hypocrite as well. They will accuse us of having used Afghanis and Angolans, Grenadians and Nicaraguans, Poles, Czechs, and others as foot soldiers and cannon fodder in our war against the Soviet Empire, only to turn our backs on them once the Soviets were defeated. If those democrats succeed with our help, though, future generations will envy us and sing our praises.

This short book is an interpretive essay and a call to action, trying simultaneously to put the events of the past two decades in their proper context and to urge the West—above all, America—to embrace the Democratic Revolution and make it the centerpiece of our international strategy. We would do well to recall Thomas Paine's words at the time of the First Democratic Revolution:

> Tyranny, like hell, is not easily conquered; yet we have this consolation with us, that the harder the conflict, the more glorious the triumph. By perseverance and fortitude we have the prospect of a glorious issue; by cowardice and submission, the sad choice of a variety of evils.

2

***

THE ORIGINS OF THE DEMOCRATIC REVOLUTION

Almost from the first, politicians, historians, and scholars have debated whether America was "revolutionary" or "conservative." Insofar as Americans think about such things at all, we tend to look at the French Revolution as the "real" revolution and our own struggle for independence from England as a far tamer affair. In fact, the American Revolution was more successful, and far more profound, than the French. Our revolution created a stable democracy, while theirs produced experiment after failed experiment for nearly two hundred years.

The American Revolution

Americans were twice pushed through a revolutionary filter: the colonists themselves were in large part people seeking greater freedom and opportunity, and even those white people who came as indentured slaves were able to earn their freedom. The population of the New World was filtered again during the revolution: between 60,000 and 100,000 royalists fled the United States (out of a total population of about 2.5 million) to Canada, England, and the Bahamas, and with very few exceptions, they did not return. As R. R. Palmer notes in his classic, *The Age of the Democratic Revolution*, "The French émigrés returned to France. The émigrés from the American Revolution did not return . . . the 'American consensus' rests in some degree on the elimination from the national consciousness, as well as from the country, of a once important and relatively numerous element of dissent."[1]

The revolutionary Americans drove out those who preferred a traditional monarchy to the revolutionary experiment, an act that has inspired the rest of the world ever since. Those revolutionaries imposed reciprocal restraints on government and the governed through "the device of the constitutional convention, which, revolutionary in origin, soon became institutionalized in the public law of the United States."[2] The revolutionary principles were typically paradoxical:

> The people, having exercised sovereignty, now came under government. Having made law, they came under the law. They put themselves voluntarily under restraint. At the same time, they put restraint upon government. All government was limited government; all public authority must keep within the bounds of the constitution and of the declared rights.[3]

The universality of the American Revolution lay in the conviction that governmental powers were derived from the consent of the governed and were therefore limited, just as personal freedom was limited by the constraints of law. Europeans had not grasped this powerful concept; indeed most European statesmen and intellectuals still believe that the state's interests are more important than those of its individual citizens. "Reason of State," so deeply ingrained in the European consciousness, is basically alien to the political philosophy of the American Constitution.

In the Age of the Second Democratic Revolution, our political philosophy and our unique historical success inspire those fighting against tyranny. To be sure, the American model is exceptional: we had an enormous advantage over Europeans, because we did not have a feudal aristocracy or feudal political-religious institutions to contend with,[4] so the creation of democracy was easier than in countries with a heavier burden of the past.[5] Perhaps because we were more fortunate than the others, ours is the fullest example of democratic revolution. By comparison, the French Revolution was a failure: first, because it passed into the hands of fanatics; second, because it collapsed internally and was captured by

Bonaparte; and, finally, because it was defeated in battle. After Waterloo came the restoration of the monarchy.

The American Revolution is often shortchanged because of a false picture of what a revolution really looks like. Like so much of contemporary culture, this too has been hijacked by the Left, which has successfully sold the notion that all revolution comes from the Left and is the result of oppression and misery. Revolution, in this view, is the product of the righteous wrath of the poor, visited upon the rapacious rich. As such, it is an act of desperation, a last shot before succumbing to the inevitable victory of the oppressors.

There were certainly moments when the poor rose up against those richer than themselves, but those moments were as likely to be counterrevolutionary as revolutionary. Indeed, some of the purest examples of spontaneous peasant uprisings against greedy bourgeois oppressors are to be found in the French counterrevolution,[6] suggesting that insurrections based on rage are not the monopoly of any single part of the political spectrum. Moreover, the most revolutionary group in history is the middle class, which is generally well-off and which engages in revolutionary activity to gain political power commensurate with its economic importance. Finally, an uprising is not necessarily revolutionary, and revolutions are not born out of despair. The greatest twentieth-century uprising—the suicidal revolt of the Warsaw ghetto during the Passover holiday in 1943—was certainly an act of desperation, but it was not revolutionary. The Warsaw Jews decided to go down fighting, taking as many Nazis with them as they could. Revolutions are entirely different: revolutions are acts of hope, seeking not only the defeat of the old regime but the creation of something different. The great Democratic Revolution of our time is an assertion of creative self-confidence.

The call for limited government, so fundamental to the American Revolution, is widely considered "conservative" nowadays, which is a tribute to the confusion that besets us. The demand to limit the power of the state is truly revolutionary, because it leaves the maximum freedom to individuals, thereby opening the future to the full range of imagination and creativity. The opposite tradition vests power in the state, and as we have seen to our sorrow, it is possible to combine radical democratic rhetoric with institutionalized terror in a "revolutionary" state regime. This lethal yet intoxicating vision was born during the Terror of the French Revolution. It has been accurately termed *totalitarian democracy,*[7] and it has found its modern expression in the totalitarian regimes of the Left and the Right in the Soviet Union, Nazi Germany, and Fascist Italy.

None of the countries emerging from tyranny during the past twenty years has demanded greater power for the central government. All, in one way or another, have insisted on the transfer of significant power from the government to the people.[8] The revolutionary events of the past twenty years are therefore "conservative" in the same way as Reagan's, Thatcher's, and Gingrich's "revolution": all seek to deprive the state of powers it previously held, to the benefit of individuals. The American Revolution provided the first consistent example of this radical transformation of the political system to the advantage of the individual, and America continues to be the inspirational force behind the Democratic Revolution.

The Democratic Revolution is as paradoxical as the America that inspires it: simultaneously radical and conservative, isolationist and global. In keeping with this dialectic, the seeds of the revolution began to sprout precisely when it seemed that the antidemocratic forces were on the verge of their greatest victory and when the West had lost confidence in its strength and in the righteousness of its cause.

Beginnings of the Revolution

As if in a Greek tragedy, the Second Democratic Revolution began at the moment of maximum Communist power and hubris and deepest democratic weakness and despair in the mid-1970s. Throughout the West, political institutions were beleaguered with scandals, from Watergate on down, and some of these—like the one involving the Lockheed Corporation—were so vast as to involve several countries.

In addition to the moral damage of the scandals, the economic structure of the industrialized world was called into doubt by the sudden, violent increase in oil prices. And, perhaps most ominously, the Soviet Union relentlessly expanded its military power and its geopolitical outreach, stretching into the Horn of Africa and Central America. With this triple-barreled assault against the

West, several leading intellectuals announced that we were facing a fundamental, structural crisis "of the system," which could be resolved only by a drastic change in the style of Western life and an equally drastic transformation of our institutions. The first generation of radical ecologists, like Barry Commoner and the members of the Club of Rome, was gravely forecasting an imminent shortage of global resources, fought over by a rapidly expanding population. The crisis was blamed on the greed intrinsic to capitalism, and their solution to this crisis was an austere socialism: central planning of the allocation of scarce resources and a global redistribution of wealth to raise up the poor and diminish the luxuriousness of the lifestyles of the well-to-do.

The Carter administration accepted and elaborated this dismal vision, as did countless Western intellectuals and politicians who were eager to blame their own countries and cultures for the misery of the third world. Inevitably, all this gloom and doom was put into the "big picture" of our continuing war with communism, and many concluded that, as Marx had predicted, the tide of history was at long last running out on the capitalist era and the West could at best ease the pain of the transition by accommodating itself to the inevitable. Even the staunchest defenders of democracy were inclined to despair; these were the years in which European bestsellers included works by Jean-François Revel about "the totalitarian temptation" and "why democracies fail."

The United States showed alarming signs of confusion and paralysis. Starting in the mid-1970s with congressional investigations spearheaded by the Church and Pike Commissions, American legislators had wallowed in public shame, exposing, dissecting, and invariably exaggerating past errors and excesses. This curious phenomenon began as a partisan Democratic attack against the Nixon administration, but it soon became assimilated into the soul of American politics. By the time Jimmy Carter came into office, many of his top advisers, from Secretary of State Cyrus Vance to Director of Central Intelligence Stansfield Turner, made contrition for past sins a central theme of American policy. The slogan "We have met the enemy and he is us" meshed nicely with American willingness to believe the unbelievable about our enemies, for both were integral parts of one of the most peculiar and most debilitating ideas of the post–World War II world: the myth of moral equivalence. Vigorously promulgated by Communist disinformation—and widely accepted in progressive circles in the West—this grotesque distortion of reality suggested that there was no fundamental moral difference between the two superpowers. We both had too many weapons, we both spied on each other and the rest of the world, we both had alcoholics and slums, and we both killed.

The likes of Professor Paul Kennedy of Yale University even argued that, of the two superpower "empires" extant in the modern world, ours was the more likely to fail because we were guilty of "economic overreach." Others, like Richard Barnet and Theodore von Laue, blamed us for the creation of something called "the national security state," argued that there was no real difference between the CIA and the KGB, and held the United States the primary villain in the cold war. Such men of the Left—like Carter's Secretary of State Cyrus Vance, who proclaimed that Carter and Brezhnev "shared common dreams"—at least had the merit of candor; for the most part the myth of moral equivalence (or, in its extreme version, the big lie that *we* were the root cause of international tension and the prime supporter of repressive regimes) passed tacitly into political discourse.

When two of the intellectual giants of the cold war period, Alexander Solzhenitsyn and Robert Conquest, wrote the truth about Stalin's monstrous crimes, their works were dismissed as fantasies, and Solzhenitsyn himself was widely written off as a religious fanatic. Accurate descriptions of the true state of affairs behind the iron curtain were denounced or censored. Accounts of the concentration camps were either greeted with silence or spiked by the leading publishers.[9] The point here is not only that Western intellectuals deceived themselves, their readers, and their students about the nature of reality—erring consistently on the side of Communist disinformation—but that this overwhelming intellectual consensus made sensible policy virtually impossible. An effective challenge to the Soviet Empire had to be based on the recognition that our society and our values were superior to theirs and therefore deserved to prevail. Once the notion that there was no moral difference between them and us was accepted, no one would likely accept the risks involved in fighting the Russian Bear.

This amazing political and moral confusion in the face of violent antidemocratic unrest in the world shattered the morale and coherence of our own leaders and reinforced the despair of our allies. Unable to distinguish between our friends and enemies, our leaders ended by adopting our enemies' view of the world.

America was divided and weakened, and our European friends took their distance from us, moving closer to the false moral equivalence so avidly preached by the Soviets and their supporters. Most of these men and women were simply being prudent, hedging their bets in case the Soviet Union won the cold war, although some acted as if they thought there was rather more merit to the Soviet position than to ours. German Chancellor Willy Brandt and Swedish Prime Minister Olaf Palme often suggested that the United States, and not the Soviet Union, was the major threat to world peace and the creation of a just society. Brandt and his henchman Egon Bahr ostentatiously adopted Soviet views on many East-West issues, and during the latter stages of the Vietnam War, Palme's government went so far as to compare the United States with Nazi Germany.

The European anti-Americanism of the 1960s and 1970s was not monochromatic; it drew upon traditions of both the Left and the Right, and while they shared resentment that we, rather than they, were the preeminent Western power, their condemnations of us were quite different. For the Left, America was hateful because it represented laissez-faire capitalism rather than the fashionable Swedish social-democratic model and because America was seen as an imperial power launching a genocidal war against brave third world peoples in Vietnam and Latin America. For the Right, America was contemptible because Americans were uncultured and because the United States seemed to lack the will to impose itself on the world at large. We were whipsawed between the two political poles, attacked as too vicious by the Left and too flaccid by the Right.

Under these circumstances, the United States was poorly placed to lead a global transition to democracy, even if our leaders had been inclined to do so (and they generally were not). Inevitably, many of our leaders shared much of the pessimism about America. Nixon had interventionist instincts, but, like Henry Kissinger, he prided himself on a strategy based on *Realpolitik;* he was not, contrary to popular belief, a vigorous ideological challenger of communism. Nixon's foreign policy was based on the conviction that the Soviet Union was strong and stable—then the dominant academic hypothesis about Soviet socialism. Nixon was also pessimistic about Americans' will to challenge the USSR after the Vietnamese catastrophe. By the time the Second Democratic Revolution had begun in Iberia, Nixon was thoroughly engaged with Watergate, the negotiations over Vietnam, and the followup to the Yom Kippur War in the Middle East. Things deteriorated further under Ford and Carter.

As we now know, the Soviet Union was in terrible economic shape even as it relentlessly built its military power. Soviet armed might actually overtook that of the West in several major categories, from missile size to the number of advanced submarines, the quantity and quality of artillery, and the effectiveness of its intelligence services. By the late 1970s, such respected institutions as the London Institute for Strategic Studies were gloomily analyzing the strategic "tilt" in favor of the East, even as the NATO countries were reducing their defense spending (and we subsequently learned from the Russians that our count of their nuclear warheads was at least 10,000 too low).

The growing power of the empire was easy to see: from Afghanistan to the Horn of Africa and Central America, Soviet influence expanded with apparent ease and alarming speed. Cuban troops moved into Africa in the wake of the departure of Western colonial rulers, the fall of Vietnam was followed by the expansion of Communist tyranny in Southeast Asia, and, for the first time, the Soviet Empire established a foothold on the American landmass, with the Sandinista seizure of power in 1979. Yet the Carter administration gave aid to the Sandinistas, perhaps hoping that Nicaraguan moderates would eventually win out.[10] This sort of wishful thinking, masquerading as geopolitics, did not inspire our friends and allies. It rather reminded them of the catastrophe that had befallen American foreign policy at the beginning of the year, when the shah of Iran had fled his country, routed by the fanatical anti-Western forces of the Ayatollah Khomeini.

The Iberian Model

Spain. The disarray and weakness of American policy in those years discouraged and confused many of those fighting on the front lines of the Democratic Revolution. In the autumn of 1977, I met with Spanish President Adolfo Suarez, who posed the question in very stark terms. "Why," he demanded, "does the United States wish me to fail?" Shocked at his question, I told him that I was certain that President Carter, indeed all Americans, were praying for his success. He laughed bitterly and snarled that Basque terrorism was the only real threat to Spanish democracy and he had warned the Americans of the terrible strains created by the terrorist onslaught. But when he asked for technical help from the CIA, it was denied, on the grounds that the Basques were "domestic," not "international," terrorists. He could not believe it. "How damned international do they have to be?" he angrily demanded. "They live in France, train in North Africa, and kill in Spain. Isn't that international enough for the Americans?"

Suarez was certainly right; the United States should have come to his aid. At that moment, history pivoted on a Spanish hinge. If democracy had been thwarted in Spain—as it had been a decade earlier in Spanish America—the door to the Democratic Revolution might not have opened for another generation, because the world would not have had the all-important model of a successful and peaceful transition from dictatorship to democracy. The Spanish (and, to a somewhat lesser degree, the Portuguese) experiences shattered the conventional wisdom, according to which dictatorships could be overthrown only by acts of violence. The Iberian transition to democracy also helped destroy the stereotype of Latins as somehow intrinsically better suited for macho dictatorship than for proper Westminster or Washington democracy.

Suarez and King Juan Carlos grasped the drama of their moment[11] and understood the importance it should have had for the citadel of democracy, the United States. How could America—particularly under the leadership of a new president proclaiming his commitment to a global campaign for human rights—fail to respond to the cries for help from the fledgling democracy in Spain? Suarez reasoned from recent American history: the Marshall Plan safeguarded the durability of democracy in Western Europe after World War II, when Soviet-sponsored communism threatened the continent. The success of Western Europe provided reliable allies and a rich market for the United States. Should there not be a second Marshall Plan for Spain, and perhaps Portugal as well, as they emerged from dictatorship and faced a rough challenge from Communists, nostalgic right-wingers, and terrorists?

To be sure, the circumstances were quite different. Western Europe was largely wrecked after the war, whereas Spain had recovered from the worst effects of the dreadful civil war of the 1930s and was firmly on the road to becoming a "normal" European country. Spain did not need the kind of massive economic assistance that the Marshall Plan had provided; that virtually the entire Spanish elite believed such an effort was necessary showed how little they understood the dynamic process of economic development, how heavily they relied on state intervention rather than private enterprise, and how important they reckoned the role of the United States. What Spain and Portugal did need—as the emerging democracies would need a decade later—was a vigorous embrace, assistance in fighting the enemies of democracy (ETA terrorists in Spain, radical Leninists in Portugal), and practical guidance in moving to democratic capitalism.

The United States ignored the call for help from Spain but did give some emergency support to the democratic forces in Portugal. Happily, both countries moved peacefully from dictatorship to democracy. Oddly, the Spanish president and the Portuguese prime minister had the same last name, even though their political traditions were quite different: the Portuguese Socialist Mario Soares successfully led the fight against the Communist Party in the streets of Lisbon, Porto, Coimbra, and Faro, while the conservative veteran of Francoism, Adolfo Suarez, opened the gates of the Spanish political system to the formerly ostracized parties of the Left. There were other, almost uncanny similarities; just as democracy in Spain was won by an unlikely coalition between a traditional politician (Suarez) and a military man (King Juan Carlos), so in Portugal Mario Soares teamed up with General Ramalho Eanes (a friend and protégé of U.S. General Alexander Haig) and other military leaders to defeat the Communists, led by one of the great Stalinists of the postwar era, Alvaro Cunhal.

Portugal. Cunhal was highly esteemed by the Soviets, and Politburo leaders in Moscow were known to believe that it was a pity a man as talented as Cunhal was "wasted on Portugal,"[12] a relatively minor country in the Soviets' struggle for Europe. But Cunhal's talents proved ill-suited to a democratic political contest. He might have succeeded in a Leninist seizure of power, but he was no match for Soares in the rough-and-tumble of electoral politics. Even so, it was a close call. The Portuguese Revolution had taken place in April 1974, led by a group of military officers determined to put an end to Portugal's colonial wars in Africa and to create a Socialist state at home. For the first year, governments succeeded one another with Italian-like frequency, until an abortive right-wing coup attempt almost exactly a year after the revolution.

Starting in the spring of 1975, the Communists and other far left groups intensified their efforts to consolidate control over the country, their sense of urgency suddenly galvanized by a national election in April that showed the Socialists were the strongest party in the country. Their basic method was to use workers' organizations to paralyze the government and opposing political parties. The Socialist newspaper *República*—the only significant newspaper in the country that was not under Communist or pro-Communist control—was shut down by a printers' strike in the spring, and Communist-controlled trade unions paralyzed the Catholic radio station. In the early summer, the radio station was blown up. It seemed strikingly like a replay of the Communists' successful seizure of power in Central and Eastern Europe after the war. But it did not work in Portugal.

The president, General Costa Gomes, was a democratic leftist who chose the moderate Pinheiro Azevedo to head the government in September. But Azevedo did not have sufficient support from the military—above all its radical wing, under the control of General Otelo de Carvalho, commander of the army special forces in Lisbon. When, in November, Azevedo could not get the military to remove some 50,000 construction workers who besieged his palace and the National Assembly for a day and a half, he submitted his resignation. This focused the spotlight clearly on Carvalho, for he had refused to send his troops to the assembly to liberate the building from the workers' siege. Costa Gomes fired him but rescinded the order the following morning in the face of broad support for Carvalho.

The country seemed headed toward civil war, with both ends of the spectrum fearing a coup from the opposite camp. Meanwhile, the government pushed ahead with nationalizations and radical land redistribution. On November 24, tens of thousands of farmers blocked roads to Lisbon, protesting Communist-led land seizures. They demanded Carvalho be removed and threatened to cut off power and water to Lisbon if President Gomes failed to act within twenty-four hours.

On the morning of the 25th, fifty radical paratroopers seized the air force command post and communication center at Monsanto and locked the commander, General Freire, in his office. In the frenzy of their actions, however, no one thought to cut off Freire's telephone, and he was able to use it to inform his colleagues what was going on and actually organize the counter-coup while technically under office arrest by the conspirators. His first order—which quickly proved decisive—was to send the bulk of the air force to the north, a firmly anti-Communist region. Meanwhile, the leftists had seized key army bases at Monte Real, Tancos, and Montijo, and another ultraleftist unit occupied several national and foreign news agencies. Still others took over the national radio, which then broadcast false reports of the coup's success.

Costa Gomes, who had fully earned his reputation as a ditherer, moved surprisingly quickly, and within thirty-six hours the leftists had been driven out of virtually all their bases, the chief conspirators were arrested, and the Communists—who had first called for vast public support, but then, once it became clear that such support was not forthcoming, had given only lukewarm public support to the coup—were humiliated. But during the 25th, Portugal was effectively divided into two countries, a division reflected in the drastically different content of television broadcasts: the north saw an old Danny Kaye movie, while the south, under pro-Communist control, saw Soviet-style gymnastics and heard military music. The morning of the 26th was decisive, as air force fighters buzzed Lisbon from their bases in the north, and the coup leaders surrendered at Tancos. It was over soon afterward.

Mario Soares said later that Cunhal had tried to repeat the Bolshevik Revolution of 1917 but that he had been deluded by his own propaganda into believing that the Communist Party enjoyed vast public support. Certainly Cunhal had few objective bases for such a belief; the party had not received even 15 percent of the votes in the April legislative elections. The Bolshevik analogy was quite right, for Lenin could not have won an election in Russia, either; he needed a coup to seize power. Soares's behavior showed that he took the metaphor quite seriously; on the 25th itself, the Socialist leader quickly moved north, to the zone occupied by anti-Communist forces, where he met safely with his domestic and foreign supporters.

The fight for democracy in Portugal was a classic cold war confrontation, with the Soviets' supporting one side and NATO the other. The democrats in Portugal found the necessary support among the European member parties of the Socialist International and, in the fullness of time, from the United States as well. The support from the Socialist International often arrived in unconventional ways. On one occasion, an official of the Dutch Labor Party (Harry van den Bergh, who was both the national security and defense spokesman of the party and the president of the Sakharov Foundation) came to Lisbon, ostensibly to cheer at a soccer match between Benfica (the Dutch team) and Ajax (the Portuguese team). Cheer he did, and so did his local friends, for he was carrying a suitcase full of hard currency for the Portuguese Socialist Party. This was just one of several transfers, usually from the Dutch, German, or British Labor Parties (the Portuguese Socialist Party was formally organized in Germany in 1973, by Portuguese émigrés living in France and England, and Willy Brandt was a sort of political godfather to Soares).[13] Such operations, combined with political advice and counsel, were often assisted by the AFL-CIO International Office, headed by the legendary Irving Brown. Despite initial reservations on the part of Secretary of State Henry Kissinger, American Ambassador Frank Carlucci—to whom a generation of Portuguese democrats owes a debt of gratitude— eventually convinced the administration that if it threw its full support behind Mario Soares and other anti-Communists, Portugal would be saved for democracy. It was easier to see from Lisbon than from Washington. Kissinger was exceedingly pessimistic and told Soares to his face that he risked going down in history as the Kerensky of the Portuguese Communist revolution. Carlucci, who, on the ground in Portugal, had a better sense of the timbre of the Portuguese democrats, sensed correctly that the great mass of the people did not want to live under communism. In the end, the democrats prevailed with a minimum of violence.

The Spanish Transition to Democracy. No such threat was mounted in Spain, for the Spanish Communists, under the leadership of Santiago Carrillo, pursued power through political means.[14] Carrillo was the leading exponent of "Eurocommunism," claiming to have accepted in full the rules of the democratic game, and he openly clashed with leaders of the Soviet Communist Party. Like the other Eurocommunists, Carrillo's embrace of democracy was not convincing, since votes within his own PCE (Spanish Communist Party) invariably verged on unanimity and "democratic centralism" remained one of the governing principles of party life.

Moreover, Carrillo had a small fortune stashed away in Romanian banks, under the watchful eye of the dictator Nicolae Ceausescu, who could hardly be considered a Western democrat. Carrillo's Romanian connection was unknown to most observers, but top Spanish government officials were well aware of it. When Suarez initiated contacts with Carrillo before the legalization of the Spanish Communist Party, he did so through Ceausescu.[15]

After Franco's death in 1975, the Spaniards amazed themselves and most everyone else by achieving a peaceful transition to democracy. The democratization of Spain was one of the most fascinating events in recent history, for it was systematically planned and executed by a king who was universally regarded as an idiot playboy and by a president who had made his entire political career in the Francoist Falange. About two years before Franco died, the king asked a handful of political leaders to give him a written plan for the future of the country following the death of the leader. On the basis of this "written exam," Juan Carlos told Suarez that, in the fullness of time, he would be called on to manage the transition. Thereafter, they stayed in regular contact, updating their political blueprint. When Suarez became president, he and the king were in full accord on what needed to be done. The success of the Spanish transition rested to a considerable degree on the reciprocal esteem and understanding between Suarez and Juan Carlos.

There were other factors at work in the Spanish transition, ranging from the very aggressive reformist role of the Catholic church—especially one of its activist movements, Opus Dei—to the unexpectedly responsible stance adopted by the Socialist Party under the leadership of Felipe Gonzalez. Perhaps most surprising of all, we must credit the legacy of the late dictator. Thanks to some exceptionally good scholarship, we know that Franco recognized that his movement and the authoritarian system he created were destined to disappear with his death, and the bulk of the evidence suggests that he was certainly not disturbed by the prospect. In his final year or two, Franco discussed the future of Spain with top members of the government, often omitting any mention of his movement. His conversations with foreign diplomats followed similar paths, as he stressed the fundamental transformation of the country in his years in power. While it would probably be an overstatement to say that Franco had consciously prepared the country for democracy, he did oversee the creation of a middle class and recognized that this process would inevitably lead to demands for liberalization, power sharing, and eventually steps toward democracy. Not only did Franco not try to prevent the evolution of Spain, but he himself arranged to grant increasing power to the emerging middle class.

As in Portugal, there was nothing inevitable about the triumph of democracy in Spain. Had Franco been determined, at all costs, to ensure the survival of his movement and the continuation of his authoritarian regime, he would have produced an intense radicalization of the Spanish polity that would have made a peaceful transition enormously more difficult and a violent confrontation far more likely. In like manner, had Spain not been so fortunate as to find exceptional leaders like the king, Suarez, and Felipe Gonzalez, the transition could very well have degenerated into a struggle of all against all. In the event, Spanish leaders—along with their Portuguese counterparts—not only brought democracy to their countries but provided a model for other parts of the world.

The Triumph of Democracy

The peaceful transition from dictatorship to democracy in Iberia was the first giant step in the Second Democratic Revolution for three reasons. First, it shattered one of the most widely believed myths of the cold war era—that only military defeat could enable a people to throw off the shackles of twentieth-century tyranny and create a free society. Second, it provided a model that others could study and adapt to their own national circumstances. In the two decades that followed, many—beginning with those countries with close cultural ties to Spain and Portugal—would emulate the Iberian democratic revolution. Third, it destroyed the myth that communism was the wave of the future.

Developments in Latin America. The Iberian democrats inspired South and Central America, showing the Left that violent, Marxist revolution was not the only route to democracy and reassuring the Right that modern Socialists need not be a threat to traditional values or good government. Latin America was unlikely to go from military dictatorship to elected democracy without the examples and the active encouragement of Portugal and Spain. Guidance and inspiration also soon came from Pope John Paul II, Margaret

Thatcher, and Ronald Reagan. Reagan's diplomats spent a lot of political capital in support of Latin American democratic institutions, warning the dictators and would-be strongmen that the United States would take a dim view of those who challenged legitimate democrats. By the mid-1980s, Reagan—through such outspoken men as Assistant Secretary of State Elliott Abrams and Ambassador Vernon Walters (whose four army stars made him an authoritative spokesman to the military men in Latin America)—had made it clear that he would not support antidemocratic regimes. This stance undoubtedly helped dissuade potential coup leaders and was probably decisive in convincing Chilean General Pinochet to submit to the verdict of his people and retire.

The combination of the Iberian transformation and U.S. pressure produced amazing results. When Ronald Reagan took office, there were only two democratically elected governments in South America: Colombia and Venezuela. Eight years later, there were only two governments in the entire region—including Central America and the Caribbean—that were *not* elected: Cuba and Suriname. This spectacular political shift has rarely been noted, in part out of reluctance to credit Reagan for revolutionary change, in part because Latin American events are not considered newsworthy in most of the American and European media, and in part because the intellectual elites have bought into the nonsense that all revolutions come from the political Left. Yet the political wisdom and courage to navigate the dangerous waters from dictatorship to democracy, and the intellectual wisdom and courage to challenge the dominant defeatist political culture, came first from the Latin countries and were attacked from both Left and Right. It is probably too soon for us to understand how and why the Catholic world found its revolutionary sea legs earlier than the Protestant nations, but it is surely no accident that a pope such as John Paul II, who understood that the world had reached a potentially historic turning point and that dictatorship might now be peacefully defeated in many parts of the world, emerged at the same time as outstanding democratic leaders all over the Latin world. It is also no accident that the Democratic Revolution began on the periphery of the Free World, where American protection could be quickly and efficiently extended to the new democracies.

Breaking the Communist Myth. The third historic consequence of the transition to democracy in Iberia was to shatter the myth that communism was the wave of the future. The Polish opposition—from Solidarity to the Underground University—systematically studied the Spanish and Portuguese cases, as did others elsewhere in the Soviet bloc. F. W. De Klerk took a careful look at how Juan Carlos had dealt with the Spanish Communist Party, in engineering the peaceful transition to democracy in South Africa. The Spanish Communist and Socialist Parties had been quickly normalized, and their leaders granted amnesties and full rights; De Klerk quickly normalized the African National Congress and released Nelson Mandela from his long imprisonment on Robin Island.[16]

The demonstration that history was not moving inexorably toward socialism marked a major sea change in the political culture of the West. Leading figures among the European and American intelligentsia had long believed that capitalism was doomed and that the laws of history were working in favor of a very different kind of society. In countries like France and Italy, one virtually had to be a Marxist (if not a member of the Communist Party) to qualify as a true intellectual, a vogue reflected in the press, movies, and school textbooks of the period. Even that great non-Marxist thinker Raymond Aron experienced considerable social ostracism. The leading newspaper, *Le Monde,* was a leftist bull session, as was *El Pais* in Spain. The Italian intelligentsia had long been under the sway of the Communist Party, and the most prestigious German intellectuals such as Gunther Grass and Heinrich Böll were likewise of the Left, although Germany, like England, maintained a vigorous and independent conservative press, most notably the *Frankfurter Algemeine Zeitung.* Here and there one found academics with differing views—above all, ex-Communists who had broken with the party in the 1950s or following the occupation of Czechoslovakia in the fall of 1968—but they were relatively rare.

The virtual hegemony of the Left over the elite culture of Western Europe anticipated by more than twenty years the apogee of the vogue of "political correctness" in the United States and had much the same effect: the creation of a political culture based on slogans rather than critical, or even factual, analysis and a generation largely ignorant of some of the basic facts about the world. For most of the postwar period, it was folly to challenge the dominant Marxist political culture, for anyone who did so was simply excluded from the salons, newspapers, cinema, and chic publishing houses. Yet, in the mid-1970s, the first cracks in the solid cultural front were opened in France and Italy by two tough-minded scholars, helped by the writings of the most famous Soviet émigré dissident.

Developments in Italy. Italy was the last European country to emerge from radical left-wing cultural domination, which is only to be expected from a country with the largest Communist Party outside the Soviet Union. The defeat of Communist ideology in Italy was not fully accomplished until the Soviet Empire had fallen, but considerable progress had been made well before the late 1980s. A great deal of the credit must go to a very wise and very brave university professor in Rome. In early 1975, I conducted a book-length interview on fascism with Professor Renzo De Felice, the leading historian of the period. The interview proved so explosive that the publisher—Vito Laterza, himself a Communist Party member—held the books in the warehouses for several weeks until the spring elections were over. Once released, it became the object of a major assault of left-wing cultural terrorism. For months, it was virtually impossible to read a newspaper, watch an evening of television, or listen to a few hours of radio without running into a supercharged attack on De Felice, not only for the presumed "errors" of his historical analysis but also for "corrupting Italian youth." More than one critic suggested that he be forbidden to teach at Italian universities.

De Felice's offense was to have challenged the Marxist orthodoxy, which then held sway over Italian political culture. The party line held that fascism had been purely a reactionary response from the upper and middle classes to the challenges of the Bolshevik Revolution and Italian communism. De Felice argued that fascism's political base lay in an emerging lower-middle class and its ideological roots in the French revolutionary tradition—the radical Jacobin doctrines that Talmon had termed "totalitarian democracy." These revolutionary Fascists were not industrialists or well-to-do businessmen defending their self-interest against left-wing radicals but members of a rising lower-middle class and a new political force in postwar Italy.

The De Felice interpretation was a deadly threat to Marxist theory, for it meant that the "revolutionary" tradition was mother to both fascism and communism and so there was no neat moral dichotomy between communism (good) and fascism (bad). Furthermore, it undermined the Communists' claim that they had been the core of the resistance to Mussolini and that the Communist Party was therefore the sole reliable judge of, and indeed the incarnation of, antifascism. After De Felice, antifascism could no longer be seen as the sole preserve of the Left. The Left had always asserted an enviable political privilege as an article of dogma: the Left and it alone, as the original anti-Fascist force, could issue certificates of political legitimacy. Anyone who challenged the Left could be effectively discredited by being labeled Fascist. In fact, however, said De Felice, Fascists and Communists shared far more revolutionary history and political ideology than they admitted. Throughout the West, it was chic to scorn anti-Communists as hopelessly reactionary, to the point where one could speak of "anti-anti-communism" as the official world view of the intellectual elite.[17] If De Felice's view prevailed, the Communists would be toppled off their political and moral pedestal; they would be seen to share a common ancestry with the Fascists.

It was a long and bitter fight, and the Left fought savagely to maintain its monopoly over interpretations of history. Similar battles were fought throughout the West—including that against "political correctness" in the United States. It is a terribly important struggle, for, as George Orwell so eloquently portrayed it, he who controls the past thereby shapes the future. In Italy, over the course of the following twenty years the enormous mass of evidence on De Felice's side swung the battle in his favor, and in the end his opponents have by and large either acknowledged the accuracy of his analysis or lost credibility with the reading public. *Interview on Fascism* has become one of the all-time Italian bestsellers and has been translated and published from Japan to Argentina, providing the intellectual underpinnings of the collapse of the Italian Communist Party, which finally occurred after the fall of the Soviet Empire. The battle over history proved to be decisive in the war for the Italian future.[18]

The lesson of the battle over Fascist historiography in Italy as elsewhere has been that if the enemies of democracy are permitted to define national history, it will be very difficult to get the politics right. The political debate in Italy provides a particularly clear-cut example of how the Marxist misrepresentation of fascism was being debunked in Europe in the 1970s and 1980s.

Developments in France. In France, the collapse of Communist ideology was also precipitated by a more truthful rendering of the recent past, but unlike Italy, the central figure was a foreigner: the Russian émigré author Alexander Solzhenitsyn, whose monumental *Gulag Archipelago* so thoroughly documented the evils of Soviet communism. By the early 1980s, French culture had become anti-Soviet, anti-Communist, and pro-American, a near-total reversal of the stereotypes of a decade before.

In the early and mid-1970s, even such a towering intellect as Raymond Aron was attacked by the Left as intellectually inadequate and morally suspect. Aron was that rarest of all modern phenomena, a relentlessly skeptical intellectual who resolutely kept his distance from all manner of philosophical and political movements. The reaction to his 1954 work, *The Opium of the Intellectuals,* prefigured what happened to De Felice a generation later. So violent and so unanimous was the attack from the Left that Aron wryly noted in his memoirs that, while the ex-Communists had managed to learn something from their errors, "the *progressistes*, in the manner of J.-P. Sartre . . . oscillated between various positions more or less close to the Communist Party, without ever having the chance to think straight or to regret their *insanités*."[19]

Aron's refusal to join the bandwagon of *gauchiste* existentialism, structuralism, and other fashionable visions led to his exclusion from the "progressive" press, and his right to remain on the faculty of the Sorbonne was openly challenged. Unafraid, Aron icily described the dominant culture of the period:

> Swearing by all that they hold sacred that their own Marxism has nothing to do with the one that Solzhenitsyn attacks, [the Marxists] continue to "Marxify" the universities, the social sciences, and the political and cultural magazines—naively convinced that their revolution will not end in the same despotism, too eagerly bent on destroying capitalist-liberal society to ask themselves what society they would build on the ruins.[20]

By now it is clear that Aron, and not his intellectual opposite, Jean-Paul Sartre, will be remembered as the major political philosopher of the postwar generation. This represents a remarkable turnabout, for throughout the postwar period, until late in the

1970s, Sartre, the Communist existentialist, was held to be not only the leading thinker but also the symbol of his generation. Yet, so thorough was the rejection of Marxism in France that Sartre has plummeted even in cultural esteem. Sartre fell with the vogue of Marxism, and Aron rose along with the Democratic Revolution. Like an ideological weathervane, the French intelligentsia pivoted with the shifting political winds and, in the late 1970s and early 1980s, produced an impressive body of literature analyzing the change that was taking place: Hélène Carrére d'Encausse's works on the imminent fall of the Soviet Empire and the explosion of ethnic nationalisms, Jean-Francois Revel's analyses of the corruption of Western intellectuals, dozens of works exposing the evils of French communism, the brilliant novels about the KGB of Vladimir Volkov, and the anti-Communist political polemics of the "new philosophers," like Bernard-Henri Levi, who explored the evils of the empire from the Soviet gulags to the murderous regimes in Southeast Asia.

Thus, by the mid-1980s, the Democratic Revolution had gathered momentum: Spain and Portugal had demonstrated that a peaceful transition from dictatorship to democracy was possible. Every government in South America was either elected, or would soon be, and most of the other governments in the region were following suit. And in Western Europe, where Marxism had dominated the political culture ever since the war, anti-Marxist historiography and political philosophy had won a few major battles.

American Policies in Central America

The Democratic Revolution could not prevail against its major enemy—the Soviet Empire—though, unless the United States demonstrated the will and the capacity to fight and win. That would happen on several fronts: Afghanistan, Angola, Grenada, and Central America. In each case, the Soviets established a beachhead, and in each case, they were either beaten or, as in Angola and Nicaragua, contained. The war in Afghanistan was undoubtedly the most important of these, but Central America was the key challenge for the United States. After all, our ability to lead the worldwide forces of freedom against the Communists depended in part on confidence that we could win, and Central America was our backyard. If we could not stop the Communist advance there, no one could take seriously a global challenge to the empire.

The facts were passed on to Reagan from the Carter administration. The Cubans—acting as Soviet surrogates—were coordinating a massive guerrilla movement based in Nicaragua and aimed against El Salvador, Guatemala, and eventually Mexico. While there was some debate over the Sandinistas' ultimate intentions, there was little doubt about their close relations with Cuba, their commitment to turning Nicaragua into a people's democracy, and their intimate working relationship with the Soviet Union. Within a few months of seizing power, the Sandinistas had given their hard-core supporters a familiar agenda:[21]

- Talk about pluralism was frankly described as a plot to deflect or at least delay potential opposition.
- Plans were revealed for the creation of "an army politicized without precedent."
- Nicaragua was explicitly described as a fully engaged player in the "world revolution."

While many Americans believed that the Sandinistas might eventually be won over to democracy, there were no such illusions in the Kremlin. In an internal report to the Central Committee of the Soviet Communist Party in March 1980, the matter was stated explicitly:

The FSLN is the political organization in power. The leadership of the FSLN judges it indispensable to create . . . a Marxist-Leninist party charged with fighting for the creation of socialism in Nicaragua. For tactical reasons taking into account the real political situation in the country and the Central American region, the leadership of the FSLN does not, for the moment, declare publicly its final goals.[22]

An agreement was signed in Moscow five days later, and by the end of the year—at a time when Jimmy Carter was in the White House and the United States was giving substantial aid to Nicaragua—the Soviet Union was providing the Sandinistas with "special training" for up to one hundred activists per year.

Within three years, the Sandinistas had amassed the largest and most powerful army in Central America, and the internal repression—particularly of the Catholic church—was well underway, under the expert control of the Cubans. Never before had the Soviets gained a foothold on the North or Central American land mass, and we wanted to stop them before they got any closer to the Rio Grande. The point bears repetition: Reagan wanted to contain the Sandinistas, not overthrow them. The contra movement was created in an effort to thwart Sandinista arms-supply operations to the pro-Communist FMLN guerrillas in El Salvador.

Like the Sandinistas, the Salvadoran guerrillas were working closely with the Soviet Union. In the summer of 1980, Shafik Handal, the general secretary of the Salvadoran Communist Party, had written the Soviet Communist Party, asking for special training for thirty Salvadoran "comrades": six in military espionage, eight in guerrilla command, five in artillery command, five in diversionary strategy, and six in communications. The Soviets approved the request and ordered a shipment of sixty to eighty tons of "fire arms and ammunition of Western manufacture to be shipped from Hanoi via Havana for our friends in Salvador."[23]

The notion of assisting the Salvadoran government and its president, José Napoleon Duarte, was highly controversial. Even though Duarte had been duly elected and was the proponent of one of the most radical land distribution programs in all of Latin America, he was widely denounced as a man of the military right. Duarte, who fought against right-wing extremists as well as against Communist insurgents, did not live to see the happy outcome of the Central American guerrilla wars, but he earned the loyalty of a new generation of military officers and enlisted them in the fight for democracy. Many American professors, politicians, and journalists, however, simplistically equated the military with repressive intolerance, if not outright fascism.

This stereotyped presentation of the *caudillo* as the inevitable product of Latin politics was so common for so long that even some Latin Americans began to wonder if there were some sort of Latino genetic predisposition to military dictatorship. But that notion was shortsighted and factually misguided; military leaders have often played important roles in the advance of democracy. Regular army units stood fast with Yeltsin at the White House in Moscow against the attempted Communist coup in 1991; Turkish generals reestablished order and then turned the country back over to civilian rule in the 1980s; Salvadoran generals and colonels guaranteed the land redistribution scheme of Duarte against the intense rage of the Right in the late 1970s and early 1980s; and

Juan Carlos of Spain—the product of a very traditional military education—fought hard to advance democracy. Our own democracy owes much to General George Washington.

Duarte's government was well worth defending. Indeed, the threat to America from the Cubans and Sandinistas warranted giving support even to a nasty regime; despite propaganda to the contrary, El Salvador was not that. The CIA was asked to organize a "harassing" group that would interdict the air and sea supply routes. There was no intention to create a large military force that could threaten the Sandinista regime itself, because Congress—particularly Tip O'Neill's House of Representatives—would never have approved such a thing. O'Neill himself was very supportive of some of the radical Catholic groups (particularly the Maryknoll Order) that supported the Sandinistas and some of the guerrilla movements in the region.

Secretary of State Alexander Haig opposed the contra program, warning in several White House meetings that it would be "too small to succeed, but too big to hide" and that the resulting scandal would eventually lead to the abandonment of the contras by the United States, which would be the worst of all possible outcomes. Haig was half right: the contras succeeded beyond anyone's wildest expectations. The CIA started out to form a small band of marauders, a harassment group, and ended up with a popular mass movement. This result caused no end of difficulty with congressional oversight committees. They had approved the small operation and were shocked by the popularity of the anti-Sandinista movement, especially when the Sandinistas were enjoying radical chic status among American media elites and fashionable senators and congressmen. The contras soon made it clear that they did not intend to limit their efforts to saving El Salvador; they wanted to retake their own country.

At the height of its power, the Sandinista movement that overthrew General Anastasio Somoza in 1979 amounted to about 5,000 cadre; the contras reached more than 15,000 by the mid-1980s, and their success can be measured not only by the situation on the ground but also by the transformation of the political debate within the United States. At the outset, the issue was the survival of the Duarte government; at the end, the question was the survival of the Sandinista regime.

In a normal world, such success would be welcome, but the

Democratic majority in the Senate was bound and determined to keep the program within the narrow limits originally established for it. Some acted from a combination of partisan politics and myopic legalism; others bought the disinformation that the Sandinistas were a true, indigenous revolution.

To be sure, part of the problem was of the administration's own making, for the contra policy was too clever by half. The original objective was reasonable enough, but once the contras had demonstrated their strength and the evils of the Sandinistas had been documented, it was disingenuous to continue to claim that we were only defending El Salvador. It had become possible to take the revolution to the heart of the Communist regime in Managua. The contras were a genuine mass movement, entitled to our full support. Reagan certainly understood this, but at least three of his closest advisers—Michael Deaver, Jim Baker, and Nancy Reagan—believed the Central American policy to be bad politics and resisted all efforts to give more support to the contras. Nonetheless, Reagan should have taken the Central American issue directly to the public, saying, "Congress won't give me the money we need to keep the contras fighting; vote for my candidates so I can continue the fight." If he had lost, he could have blamed the Democrats for the consequences. If he had won, he would not have had to resort to such unfortunate improvisations as Oliver North's gang that rarely shot straight. Either way, the country would have had the kind of debate that serious policy issues deserve.

Although Reagan was unable to defeat the Sandinistas on their own turf, he thwarted their efforts to export Cuban-style communism to other countries in the region. And as Central America became part of the political debate in other Latin American and European countries, much of Reagan's policy was, in contrast to received opinion within the United States, generally appreciated, with leading European Socialists like Mario Soares and Felipe Gonzalez acknowledging that Reagan was right to confront Nicaragua. Felipe Gonzalez, in Washington after a trip to Central America, once commented that we might actually have underestimated the threat from the Sandinistas. "The biggest problem in Central America," he proclaimed, "is the militarization of Nicaragua." The issue eventually split the Socialist International, as Willy Brandt furiously announced at a meeting in 1982.

American policy in Central America was sufficiently success-

ful to convince the world that we were serious, that we were willing to fight, and that our enemies would not prevail. It was not a
glorious victory, but, combined with the great global surge of democracy in Iberia and elsewhere in Latin America, it added to the
awesome momentum of the Democratic Revolution, now aimed
at the Soviet Empire itself.

3

❖

HIGH TIDE OF THE REVOLUTION— THE END OF THE SOVIET EMPIRE

The collapse of the Soviet Union, Martin Malia has taught us, "was a brusque collapse, a total implosion, of a sort unheard of in history: a great state abolished itself utterly—in a matter of weeks— and right from under its president."[1] The collapse of Soviet communism and its empire must be understood as one step in the long march of the Second Democratic Revolution, some seventeen years after it began in Portugal, sixteen years after the death of Generalissimo Francisco Franco in Madrid. Moreover, the end of Soviet communism came only after the empire had visibly rent itself asunder, with Poland fallen to Solidarity, Czechoslovakia in the hands of—of all things!—an actor-playwright turned politician, the great East German hemorrhage having washed away the Berlin Wall, and the loyal tyrant Ceausescu long cold in his grave.

By the time the bell tolled for Mikhail Gorbachev, it had already tolled for many fallen dictators, from Iberia to Latin America and throughout the old empire. Each national movement drew strength and courage from those that had succeeded, of which the most important was the survival and eventual victory of Solidarity in Poland. And precisely because the Polish case was so important, the Polish pope—one of the most politically influential popes in history—played a pivotal role.

The Role of Pope John Paul II

When Cardinal Karol Wojtyla became Pope John Paul II, Giancarlo Pajetta, an Italian Communist leader with decades of experience with Poland, grimly remarked, "At least our Polish comrades won't have him breaking their balls any more." The Italian Communists knew their man, but Pajetta's optimistic prediction of Wojtyla's departure from Polish politics was totally mistaken. Not only did Pope John Paul II remain a driving force in Central European politics, but he became one of the leaders of a global crusade against communism wherever it held sway. He had carefully studied Communist methods and even before coming to Rome had advised his Italian brothers on how to deal with the subtle tactics the Italian Communist Party had adopted to divide the Catholic world. More than a year before Wojtyla's election, the Italian Communist leader Enrico Berlinguer had written a letter to an Italian bishop, suggesting the opening of a dialogue on religious questions. Carefully timed to coincide with an international bishops' synod at the Vatican, the letter came to the attention of hundreds of leading Catholic theologians, as well as the patriarch of Venice, Albino Luciani, soon to become Pope John Paul I. Luciani wrote a brief account of his experiences the day following the publication of Berlinguer's letter:

> Careful!—I was told by a Polish bishop—this is a classic move. We know it very well: they do everything possible to split the episcopate. Once a tiny crack is opened, they slip in a wedge and open the fissure. You Italian bishops are the most exposed, and they already try to portray you as anti-historical and pre-conciliar. Should one of you separate himself ever so slightly from the group, and hint ever so subtly at esteem—even with considerable doubt—for the Communist Party, what will happen? He will immediately receive the unanimous approval and affection of democratic Catholics, Christians for Socialism, and the readers of the Left-wing press. The Polish episcopate has fought against this tactic with iron com-

pactness: it has been, and it remains, our great strength.[2]

The Polish bishop was Wojtyla, and he carried into his own papacy the conviction that there could be no moral compromise with communism. He showed his determination early in his papacy by challenging "liberation theology" in Latin America. In January 1979, the pope traveled to a meeting of left-wing Latin American bishops in Puebla, Mexico. The meeting revolved around the question of whether the bishops should get involved in Marxist-inspired political activity, particularly on behalf of the poor. The pope was categorical in his rejection of the doctrine: "This idea of Christ as a political figure . . . as the subversive man from Nazareth, does not tally with the church's catechesis."[3] And in 1982, John Paul II sent a blistering letter to the Nicaraguan bishops, denouncing the "Popular Churches" in exceedingly strong language:

> A "Popular Church" opposed to the Church presided over by the legitimate pastors is—from the point of view of the teaching of the Lord and of the Apostles in the New Testament and also in the old and recent teaching of the solemn magistery of the Church—a serious deviation from the will and the plan of salvation of Jesus Christ.[4]

The Marxist regime in Nicaragua blocked publication of the letter for several weeks—as a radical priest was replaced by the bishops—but the pope was not about to let the Sandinistas dictate the terms of public debate about the role of the church in a revolutionary society. He came to Managua in March 1983 to the evident discomfiture of the regime. In the open space where he celebrated mass for half a million people, there was not even one cross; instead were pictures of Sandinista heroes and of Marx and Lenin. During his homily, the loudspeakers in the park broadcast patriotic songs, and Sandinista leaders in the front rows constantly interrupted the pope with cries of "power to the people" and "we want peace!" But John Paul was not intimidated. Upon his arrival at Managua airport, when the minister of culture, the priest Ernesto Cardenal, knelt to kiss his ring, the pope shook his finger in Cardenal's face and told him that he had better put his spiritual affairs in order.

The pope—no apologist for the capitalist West—frequently challenged the premises of Reaganism and Thatcherism (although his understanding and appreciation of democratic capitalism increased over the years), but he clearly regarded communism as the major evil of our time. Contrary to some of the fanciful claims that have appeared in print, there was no intimate working relationship between the Reagan administration and the Vatican; indeed, at the one meeting between Reagan and the pope, the president fell asleep. But there was a definite convergence of interests among the three leading world figures—Reagan, Thatcher, and the pope: all three wanted to see communism fall, and all believed it was possible to bring down the Soviet Empire without a global conflagration.

This is not to say, as so many have, that John Paul saw his mission in political terms. Rather, he realized that his religious mission would have political consequences, and he did not shrink from them:

> His leadership would put the *Ostpolitik* of the Holy See into the more comprehensive context of his worldwide campaign for human rights. He would be a disciplined witness; but he would not avoid the hard questions and the confrontations. He would insist on nonviolence; but he would also insist on the truth. The truth, he believed, would set men free in the deepest sense of human freedom.
>
> Thus, he would be, in his own way, a revolutionary. But the revolution to which he called his people would be the final revolution, the revolution of the spirit. As for the rest, the politics of freedom, God would take care of that, in God's good time.[5]

Serious policy makers almost never base their decisions on a single element of analysis, and the advisers around the pope were quite sophisticated in designing long-term strategies.[6] John Paul II himself, however, based his policies on a remarkably clear and straightforward concept of the historical moment and the role he wanted to play. The pope recognized that there are moments and circumstances in which even the most heroic actions are destined to fail, when the forces of evil are in the ascendant, or when the forces necessary to confront evil are not prepared, or not strong enough, to confront it. This was not such a time: tyranny, even Communist tyranny, was in crisis, and the pope believed that the actions of single individuals could have enormous effects. Therefore, the motivation of such people was of paramount importance, and John Paul saw his own role in precisely that context: he was to serve as the prod, the catalyst, the stimulus, or the inspiration for the people whose actions would bring about the end of communism and, he hoped, a better world thereafter. His slogan said it all: "Be not afraid."

This was also the framework for his policy with regard to the United States. Many beliefs united the Vicar of Rome and the American president. Like Reagan, John Paul II saw that the evil empire was not a solid structure at all, but a fragile edifice riddled with fault lines. And, like Reagan, the pope believed that history was the outcome of the actions of free men and women, not the result of the interplay of vast, impersonal forces. But, contrary to some of the fanciful accounts in the popular press, no joint action plan bound together Ronald Reagan and Pope Wojtyla. In fact, the pope disapproved of certain American actions and certainly disagreed with Reagan's belief in the unmitigated wonders of capitalism. Like many Catholic leaders before him, this pope (particularly in the early years of his papacy) was deeply suspicious of the materialistic basis of the capitalist vision, and he was not about to call for the replacement of one materialist system with another. This is not to say that he considered communism and capitalism morally equivalent; he well recognized the moral superiority of democratic capitalism, but he resolved to try to channel American energies by inspiring, guiding, and even manipulating people, not reaching covert agreements with the president of the United States.

Some assumed that the new pope, coming as he did from a Communist country, represented a figure of compromise with communism. This was a misunderstanding of how the church functions, however: a papal conclave is not the same thing as an American political convention. The conclave had just barely failed to elect one of the most intensely anti-Communist Italian bishops the ballot before Wojtyla's election, and the cardinals were not about to change their worldview in a matter of a few hours. John Paul II unhesitatingly set an example in confronting communism, from the vogue of liberation theology in Latin America, to Nicaragua, the first Communist regime in Central America, and of course his native Poland. In a speech in Gdansk in 1987, he used the word *solidarity* over and over again, as he had as early as 1983, and its contemporary political significance was unmistakable:

> This word, *solidarity*, we must pronounce with strength in the name of the future of man and of humanity. As a great wave today it expands across all regions of the world, conscious of one truth: that we cannot live according to the principle of "all against all," but only according to the opposite principle of "all with all," "all for all." This word we pronounce here with a new value and in a new context. The world cannot pretend not to have heard.

The pope, convinced that the Soviets had been behind the effort to assassinate him, was flabbergasted at the American government's skepticism. The pope had sent a message to Brezhnev, warning the Soviets that if the Red Army went into Poland to crush Solidarity, they would have to deal with the pope himself, in first person.[7] As Zbigniew Brzezinski would later remark, it required an act of religious faith to believe that the Kremlin was *not* involved in the operation.

The Soviets, who had good reason to fear John Paul II, would have been greatly relieved had he departed the scene. One day in the mid-1980s, the Italian satirical magazine *Il Male* produced a picture-perfect phony issue of the leading Polish newspaper, with banner headlines proclaiming: "Wojtyla Elected King of Poland." Thousands of copies were smuggled into Poland in one of the most brilliant practical political jokes of modern times. The Italian pranksters captured in five words the essence of the Polish political crisis, for the source of real political authority in Poland rested in Rome, not Warsaw. This was no laughing matter for the Soviet Empire.

It seemed clear to many in the Reagan administration that if the Kremlin could not find a solution to the Solidarity crisis, the entire empire could very well collapse.[8] Solidarity was not merely a challenge to the Polish government but a challenge to communism itself. When the Kremlin failed to destroy Solidarity, it showed a fatal, and largely unsuspected weakness, thereby unleashing the whirlwind that swept away the Soviet Empire. And that whirlwind was more than a secular political storm: it had deep Catholic roots and visible support from the throne of St. Peter. This highly politicized pope told the ambassadors to the Holy See in 1982 that the Yalta line dividing Europe into two opposing blocs was illegitimate: "Every people must have the right to determine its own destiny. The Church cannot fail to give its full support to the defense of these principles."

Looking back on the destruction of the Soviet Empire a decade later, in the encyclical *Centesimus Annus,* the pope wrote that most people believed that the Yalta order could be ended only by another war, but instead it was achieved by the nonviolent commitment of men who, "while they refused to surrender to the power of force, each time knew how to find effective ways to present the truth. This disarmed the adversary, because violence needs to legitimize itself with the lie, to assume, albeit falsely, the aspect of the defense of a right or a response to another's threat." In fact, he pointed out, the notion that a Communist regime could be removed only by force and violence was itself a Marxist myth:

> While marxism held that . . . one could only arrive at a solution of the social contradictions through violent confrontation, the struggles which produced the fall of marxism tenaciously insisted upon travelling the road of negotiation, of dialogue, of testimony to the truth.

Yet even this brave and determined man had his moments of doubt, and he was not so dogmatic as to abjure the occasional tactical retreat. In 1983, for example, he made a deal with General Jaruselski, and instead of a public meeting with Solidarity leader Lech Walesa, the pope received him in private. In this way, Jaruselski was spared the threat that a public meeting—in which the pope would have been seen to embrace the Solidarity leader—would inspire another wave of anti-Communist agitation. The pope's compromise was accurately reported in *l'Osservatore Romano,* in a piece signed by its editor, Virgilio Levi: "Not everyone will agree. On the contrary, in Poland, hardly anyone. And they will suffer for it. But there were reasons of force majeur. We honor the sacrifice of Walesa." It was not one of the pope's great moments—and the grim significance of Levi's words was quickly gainsaid by the Vatican—but it was the exception to a rule of rigorous resistance.

The pope was an indispensable component of the explosive mixture that blew communism sky-high at the end of the 1980s.

Not only did he bring his own enormous personal charisma to the side of the Democratic Revolution, but he lent the prestige and in some cases the wealth of the church to the democratic struggle.[9] It was only appropriate, after all, since the model for the peaceful transition to democracy had come from Catholic Spain, even before there was a Polish pope. Yet the democratic explosion would not have been sufficiently powerful to destroy the empire without several other ingredients, from the military defeats and containment in Afghanistan, Grenada, Nicaragua, and Angola to some other effective policies by the Reagan administration and its international allies. And even all these might not have sufficed, were it not for the providential failure of nerve of the Soviet ruling elite—above all, the seemingly limitless incompetence of Mikhail Gorbachev. These were the key components of the moment that the pope accurately defined as one in which individual actions would be decisive.

The Nature of the Crisis

Despite the conventional wisdom, chanted like a mantra over and over again, according to which "no one" foresaw the impending doom of communism, Reagan's foreign policy was based on the conviction that the Soviet Empire was doomed and would fall sometime in the near future, if we could deliver only one or two effective blows. Several top officials in the Reagan administration well understood what was going on. It was obvious, for example, that the empire's hard-currency resources were minuscule compared with its requirements. Previous empires had taken raw materials from the colonies, produced finished goods, and exported them for profit. The Soviet Empire was the opposite: the Soviet Union exported raw materials and imported finished goods, even from such colonies as the Central European satellites and Kazakhstan. The great bulk of Soviet hard-currency income came from the sale of oil, gas, gold, and diamonds. The only major industrial export was weapons. The Soviet Union was therefore an anomaly, both historically and economically: a military empire based on a third-world country that could not compete in the world marketplace, with a hopeless economic system at the mercy of commodity prices. A brief respite occurred in the mid-1970s, with the vertiginous rise of oil prices, but the long ride down, as oil prices sank below the levels prior to the runup, was devastating. Reagan understood the force of the oil weapon, which is why his administration devoted so much time and energy to convincing the Saudis to accelerate the crash by increasing their production.

By 1987, the Kremlin's hard-currency income was a pitiful $30–35 billion and dropping, and nearly one-third of that came from West European and Japanese *credits,* rather than from the sale of Soviet products and raw materials. This income would not suffice for countries much smaller than the Soviet Union. There was no way that the Kremlin could maintain the empire on this miserable cash flow. The Kremlin's foreign lenders understood that the empire was not a very good credit risk, and even the West Germans had made major reductions in their loans. At the end of 1988, the Japanese declined to participate in future lending programs.

Declining Quality of Life. The misery of daily life was also well documented. The celebrated émigré dissident Jacques Amalric conducted an interview with the émigré poet Vadim Kozovoy in *Le Monde* in late 1990, which gave a nightmarish vision indeed:

> In some cities the communal services barely function and heating is threatened. Rats jump out at you. Gasoline is lacking, economic ties between regions become ever more problematic . . . more than one hundred cities are declared zones of ecological misery. In the cities of Aralsk, the plague begins to spread. Criminality is mounting everywhere, and armed bands appear.[10]

In the same period, Andrew Nagorski of *Newsweek* interviewed Muscovite doctors, and they informed him, to his astonishment, that they had stopped prescribing medicines manufactured in the Soviet Union, on the grounds that their patients had a better chance of recovery if they took nothing at all than if they ran the risk involved in taking a Soviet product.

Then, of course, there was the anecdotal evidence of the disillusionment of the people: Soviet humor. The giveaway on Gorbachev was a very popular joke, which emerged within months of the proclamation of *glasnost:*

> A man walks into a bar and orders a beer. "One ruble, please," says the bartender.

"What? It's always been 50 kopeks," says the man.

"Da, but that was before *glasnost*. Now you pay 50 kopeks for the beer, and 50 kopeks for the *glasnost*." So what could he do? The man put a ruble on the table, and the bartender took it, went away, and came back with 50 kopeks and an empty glass.

"What's going on?" demanded the customer.

"We're out of beer, you see, so you only have to pay for the *glasnost*."

The Russians knew a failed system when they saw one.

Industrial Failures. It was also well established that Soviet industry was in a parlous state and that the Kremlin could not possibly compete with the West in advanced military technology, like the Star Wars missile defense system. Many have written that Reagan's decision to pursue Star Wars was a tactic to threaten the Soviets with bankruptcy if they attempted to compete with us, and no doubt the idea of luring the Soviets into a ruinous competition was attractive. But the Star Wars decision was also influenced by our knowledge of the systematic failures of the Soviet military-industrial complex. It might be assumed that such sensitive information was collected by secret agents, but in fact some of it came from scholarly research, both by private scholars and by government employees. One study for the Pentagon's internal think tank, the Office of Net Assessments, found that when advanced technology was transferred from the free world to the Soviet bloc, productivity dropped an average of 40 percent, regardless of the endeavor: from Italian automobiles to French chemicals, once a turnkey factory passed over the Yalta line, it produced only 60 percent as efficiently as it did back home. The reasons were well known, if sometimes ignored: rampant alcoholism, the total lack of meaningful incentives for the work force, chronic shortages of basic materials, and repeated breakdowns of machinery.

As we looked at the structural problems of the empire, it became apparent that the Communist system suffered from a peculiar kind of disconnect, almost as if there were a missing link in its nervous system. While Russia had long produced some of the world's finest mathematicians, natural scientists, and engineers, the Soviet Union was strikingly deficient in know-how. While its engineers could certainly compete with their counterparts in the

West, the Soviet industrial complex could not manufacture the same quality and quantity of products. So advanced was this "disease" that it was impossible to find a single case in which a Western turnkey factory had been modernized by the Soviets. Whenever they wanted to upgrade a product, the Soviets called the Western company from which they had bought the factory in the first place and asked it to install a new assembly line. When the Italians, for example, built the famous Fiat factory in Togliattigrad in the mid-1960s, the Soviets copied every last detail of the home factory in Turin, down to the organization of the workers on the shop floor. When, a decade later, the Italians suggested that it might be a good idea to produce newer models, they were asked to do the work themselves.

This was only the latest version of a well-established pattern. In a valuable three-volume work written a quarter-century ago, Anthony C. Sutton showed in detail that at the very start of its existence, the Soviet Union was provided with basic technology from the West: in the 1920s and early 1930s, "Germany alone built for the USSR seventeen artillery factories, all of its submarines, and plants to produce warplanes and tanks."[11] As Vladimir Bukovsky points out, this means that "literally all the industrial complexes and major factories were built by foreign firms, sometimes using foreign credit and even foreign manpower. These were the very projects touted as the great accomplishments of socialism both at home and abroad."[12] Thus, the Soviet system was heavily—fatally—dependent on Western know-how, which suggested that we might be able to put enormous pressure on the empire by restricting its access to our products and manufacturing techniques.

Indeed, other information showed even greater dependency, particularly in the strategically sensitive areas of advanced military technology. Since the Soviets were unable to match some advanced Western technologies, they either had to buy or steal them, and their financial plight made theft the more attractive option, as was demonstrated in one of the most fascinating spy stories of the cold war. Late in the Carter presidency, a French businessman in Moscow was approached on the street by an old acquaintance, a Russian who had served as commercial attaché in the Soviet Embassy in Paris. They arranged another meeting, at which time the Russian took the Frenchman through a series of quick trips on the underground and finally sat him down in a park and explained that he was a KGB official, assigned to a special, top-secret directorate tasked to steal Western technology for the Soviet military. He was, he said, sick of the Communist system and wanted to help the West. He was prepared to provide the French government with considerable documentation about the KGB's technological espionage, and he gave the Frenchman some sample documents on film.

The Frenchman returned to Paris and informed the French authorities. After studying the documents and analyzing the problem, the French used the businessman as the contact with the Russian. Once it was up and running, the operation—and the Russian—were code-named "Farewell." Although it ran for only about six months, Farewell produced spectacular results. The French government obtained thousands of secret KGB documents, detailing both the Soviets' technological espionage networks in Western Europe and the United States and the specific targets the Soviet military wanted them to obtain.

Farewell might have gone on for some time, had it not been for his amorous proclivities. Out in his car with his mistress one winter day, Farewell was surprised by a peeping Tom, and something snapped. Apparently convinced she had betrayed him, Farewell stabbed his mistress over and over again, finally throwing her bleeding body into the snow and driving off. And then, like a character in a B movie, he returned to the scene, just in time to see her being lifted on a stretcher. She opened her eyes, saw Farewell, and pointed to him, crying out, "There he is!" Arrested and jailed for attempted murder, he apparently wrote a letter to his wife in which he said, "What a shame this had to happen just now, when I was working on something very important." The KGB read the letter, wondered what he was talking about, and then tortured him until he confessed. He was executed shortly thereafter.[13]

The Farewell Legacy. Early in Reagan's first term, French President François Mitterrand told Reagan about Farewell, and the French gave the CIA a complete set of the documents. By a sort of "reverse engineering," the American experts were able to figure out the problems the Soviets were trying to solve, thereby identifying the weakest links in the Soviet military apparatus and enabling the United States and France to work together either to block the Soviet spies or to permit Soviet agents to steal technology that had

been sabotaged. The Farewell documents, which provided a rare and devastatingly accurate picture of the inner workings of the Soviet military and its friends in the intelligence business, were a big reason for the effectiveness of Reagan's policies: we knew exactly which crucial items to protect or sabotage.

We also learned a great secret, perhaps *the* fatal secret about the Soviet Empire: it could not compete with the West in the design and development of modern technology. It followed that if we could keep advanced technology out of Soviet hands, we could gain a decisive military advantage. This was in fact the pattern of the Reagan years, for the United States led a global effort to deprive the Soviet bloc of advanced technology. At home, we got serious about export controls (Carter's people had committed exactly four customs agents to the task of monitoring strategically sensitive exports; by the end of the Reagan years there were thousands of them at work), and internationally we energized the little-used Coordinating Committee for Multilateral Export Controls (COCOM). The effort, managed through the Pentagon, was so effective that, by the end, top Russian officials did not let a day go by without pleading for the abolition of COCOM. From Gorbachev and Shevardnadze on down, they all realized that unless the export-control mechanism were destroyed or at least mitigated, any hope of competing with us was doomed.

The Reagan Doctrine

Clearly, sooner or later a reckoning would come for the Soviet Empire. We believed that Judgment Day could be speeded up by challenging the Soviets on the fringes of the empire, where they were overextended.[14] This conviction produced the Reagan Doctrine: sustained support for anti-Soviet movements, from Central America to Angola and Afghanistan, demonstrating that the course of world history was not running in favor of communism and also showing the peoples of the empire that Soviet military power could be successfully challenged. As Soviet military prestige came under assault, people around the world began to think that time might be on *our* side after all.

Reagan's foreign policy, of course, was not a work of art. Enough errors were committed to fill a good-sized volume. The policy of export control was achieved only through bloody internal battles, violently opposed by some of Reagan's own cabinet members, from Secretary of Commerce Baldridge to Chief of Staff Baker, by doorkeeper Michael Deaver, and on some occasions by Secretary of State Shultz. And even the so-called Reagan Doctrine of support to anti-Communist guerrilla movements—above all in Afghanistan and Angola—owes its success as much to congressional leaders (both Democrats and Republicans) as to the Reagan appointees. Reagan's style of government was designed to let the cabinet make the key decisions whenever possible and to have the president intervene only when cabinet members could not resolve matters among themselves. This approach looks better in theory than it works in practice, especially with a president who was rarely inclined to be a taskmaster. As competing factions fought each other for the president's limited attention, policy was often paralyzed, awaiting Reagan's intervention.

Yet with all that, Reagan's policies were much better than what came before and what came after. And they were crafted despite mounting confusion among the cultural and political elites—the opinion makers. An effective challenge to the Soviet Empire had to be based on the recognition that our society and our values were superior to theirs and therefore deserved to prevail. The widespread acceptance by the elites of the false notion that there was no significant moral difference between them and us made it difficult for the American people to accept the risks involved in fighting the Russian Bear. On this point, Reagan was superb. From his "evil empire" speech to his countless recitations of the superiority of Western values and the capitalist system, he constantly attacked the Soviets at their weakest point and gave heart to those who fought the notion of moral equivalence.

Even during the Reagan and Thatcher years, however, when these two great leaders clearly enunciated the superior values of democratic capitalism, a shocking number of American analysts—in and out of government—strained to give the Kremlin the benefit of most every doubt. CIA estimates of Soviet military spending, as we now know from the Russians themselves, were exceedingly low. Even the staunchest hawks never came close to assessing the real level of Soviet military preparations. The official estimates placed Soviet defense spending at about 14–15 percent of GNP, but the actual figure was somewhere between 25 percent and 40 percent. CIA analyses of the Soviet economy were embarrassingly optimistic, and even in the last heavy breaths of the Gorbachev era, when every inhabitant of the empire knew the system was on its last legs, the CIA was forecasting steady economic growth of around 2 percent (and was predicting a long and stable tenure for Gorbachev).

The East German economy, from whose miseries millions of people fled the minute the border was open, was ranked one of the ten most successful in the world, challenging West European countries.[15] The United States was even willing to compromise its strategic security just to give the Soviets a chance to prove their good intentions. In one of those decisions that future historians will strive mightily to explain, we actually stopped developing new intercontinental ballistic missiles in the 1970s, permitting the Soviets to catch up and eventually pass us in the quantity—and often quality—of ICBMs. American withdrawal from the missile race was justified by a theory known as the "apes on a treadmill," which held that the nuclear arms race would continue so long as the United States held strategic superiority. If only parity could be achieved, the two apes would stop running. The unstated premise of this fantasy was that the Soviet Union was entitled to be as strong as we were. That theory lasted until Jimmy Carter discovered that the Soviets were not satisfied with parity: they wanted superiority. Faced with an imminent, drastic inversion of the strategic balance, Carter's last budget began the surge in American defense spending that carried through Reagan's first term.

Western Gullibility

Perhaps the ultimate example of Western gullibility was the case of Romania. Governed by a megalomaniacal killer who installed a totalitarian system so paranoid that the state kept track of women's menstrual cycles and the typeface of every typewriter in the country, Romania nonetheless came to be hailed throughout Western Europe and the United States as an example of independent, liberal communism. Ceausescu's independence from Moscow was accepted without question by most Western leaders, and as late as the mid-1980s, even the CIA was prepared to certify that we could trust a Romanian promise not to reexport advanced technology to the Soviet Union.

In reality, *all* advanced technology that reached the Romanians went on to the Soviet Union, and the program to convince the West—above all, the United States—to accept Ceausescu's "independence" was a brilliant disinformation campaign designed to facilitate Romania's access to Western technology and credits. The campaign succeeded: starting with Richard Nixon, every American president embraced the notion of a feisty little Romania that stood up to the Soviet Union. Ceausescu came to be considered the Gorbachev of his day, the kind of Communist "we can do business with." So the Romanian intelligence service was able to operate where the KGB could not tread, and the Romanians made off with such delicate NATO secrets as the blueprints for the Leopard tank. The truth about the Ceausescu regime was brought to us by the highest-ranking intelligence official ever to defect to the West from the Soviet bloc: Ion Mihai Pacepa, the acting director of the Romanian secret intelligence service and personal adviser to the dictator. His book, *Red Horizons*, is a classic, testifying not only to the horrors of the regime but to the humiliating deception of America during the presidency of Richard Nixon and long thereafter.

The only way to understand the empire is to view it as a system; with the exception of extraordinary men like Stalin, the personality of the leader had little to do with the policies of the Kremlin. Yet, so eager was the West to find evidence that the Soviets were becoming more and more "liberal" that we carefully studied each new dictator for signs of benign intentions. Even Reagan often sounded as if he believed the grave problem of the Soviet Union could be reduced to the person of Gorbachev. This error was swallowed whole by George Bush and James Baker. Gorbachev charmed the world and managed to acquire a solid political base— outside his own country. Both Reagan and Thatcher were entranced by him, and, in his final days, when his support within the Soviet Union had all but disappeared, Gorbachev could count on near-total support from the leaders of the major Western powers. If his job had depended on popularity in the West, Gorbachev would have been president for life. But his own people understood him better than the Western leaders did.

Gorbachev was the political protégé of Yuri Andropov, the first Soviet dictator to realize in great detail the gravity of the structural crisis of the Soviet system. Andropov knew this because, as head of the KGB for more than fifteen years, it had been his job to prevent the Soviet peoples from demonstrating their hatred for Soviet communism. Recently obtained documents from the Soviet Politburo show that the "dissident" movement in the mid-1970s was much stronger than most people in the West imagined, and Andropov repeatedly warned his colleagues of the seriousness of the situation. To counter the rising tide of hatred from the Soviet peoples, Andropov launched the first version of *glasnost* by calling for a reform of communism.

The undertaking was doomed from the outset, because communism cannot be reformed. It is not known whether Andropov's call for "reform" was a repeat of the deception of "détente"[16] or whether the Politburo was convinced that things were so desperate they had no choice but to attempt to reshape the system. The sensational disinformation campaign masterminded by the KGB, which convinced the Western intelligentsia that Andropov was a "closet liberal," suggests the former hypothesis. In any event, though, Andropov died before the absurdity of the mission was revealed. Faced with the choice between "reform" and reversion to the previous methods, the Politburo was unable to decide and selected Chernenko—whose health was bad enough to guarantee a very short tenure—as interregnum ruler. By the time he died, less than a year later, the Politburo had opted for "reform."

Gorbachev was then selected as the man best qualified to carry out the Andropov program. The two shared more than a worldview. As Andropov's protégé, Gorbachev derived much of his power from the KGB. Moreover, as in the case of Andropov, there is much mystery about Gorbachev's *glasnost*. Vladimir Bukovsky argues in his recent book, *Judgment in Moscow*, that Gorbachev's concessions were tactical and that he envisaged *glasnost* and *perestroika* as ploys with which to lure the West into a repeat of détente, in which Western capital would be provided to save the Soviet Communist elite. It may well be so, but whatever the true intentions of the Soviet leadership, the actual policies were disastrous.

The Role of Gorbachev

Gorbachev was like the hero in "The Emperor's New Clothes." Hailed as a great reformer, Gorbachev was in reality a confused man who utterly failed to understand the centrifugal forces within his own society and whose inability to carry out real reform had been abundantly demonstrated when he was minister of agriculture. Like his predecessors, Gorbachev presided over a relentless decline in the quality and quantity of agricultural products. But this was hardly surprising, since Soviet agriculture had been in free fall ever since the revolution. Gorbachev's more notable activities lay in other fields. Perhaps most surprising, he repeatedly pronounced himself amazed at the intensity of ethnic and nationalist passion, even though every sensible textbook on the Soviet Union had for years identified these as the two gravest problems facing the empire. Some Western experts, like Hélène Carrére d'Encausse, had warned that the Soviet Union might not survive into the twenty-first century, precisely because of the exponential growth of the Islamic minorities. How could the Soviet dictator not know he was sitting on an ethnic and nationalist explosion waiting for a spark?

A man so totally bereft of understanding regarding his own society could hardly be expected to have a clear vision of what needed to be done, and he had none. Indeed, at one time or another he was in favor of *all* solutions. Did he want a free market? Absolutely. Was he in favor of continued central planning? You bet. Would he decontrol the ruble? Undoubtedly, but it never happened. Totally lacking any semblance of a coherent program of real reform, Gorbachev attempted a kind of Hollywood reform of the empire by purging the old-line *apparatchiks* and replacing them with sexy, charming, trendy Communists like himself. For a while, he was like a political angel of death, bestowing a fatal embrace on every Communist leader he visited, and in short order he had installed new leaders in Hungary, East Germany, and Czechoslovakia. But, to his amazement, once the plug had been pulled on the old leaders, the people started mobilizing in support of democracy, first flooding to the West, then demanding revolution.

The great lesson of Gorbachev is that empires fall when the emperor and his ruling elite have a failure of will, not because of sheer structural failure. The Soviet economic system had failed long before, and—as Andropov's brief reign demonstrated—the Russian people and their oppressors knew that it had failed, although the people had a clearer picture of it than the tyrants at the top of the pyramid. But there was no revolt against the system so long as the leaders were prepared to use terror to maintain themselves in power, just as there was no revolt against Kim Il Sung in

North Korea, nor has there been an uprising against his son and successor Kim Jong Il or against Fidel Castro in Cuba. Each of these societies is in economic ruin, more like a medieval economy than a modern one, but the regime is solidly in place. The brief demonstration of democratic zeal against the tyranny of the gerontarchs in Beijing was swiftly crushed. The survival of totalitarian regimes depends on the will of the tyrant: when the tyrant is prepared to use the massive power of the state to defend the regime, revolution fails. Once it was clear that Gorbachev lacked the will to use terror to buttress Polish communism, the peoples of the empire realized that their moment had come and seized it. The empire would have lasted longer—and Gorbachev's rule along with it—had he sent the Red Army into Poland in the late 1980s instead of approving the participation of Solidarity in the Polish government. Once Lech Walesa's trade union became an equal partner with the Communist Party, the doom of Polish communism—and with it, that of the Soviet Union itself—was sealed. When the first, only partially free elections were held in Poland, the Communists did not win a single seat.

There are two kinds of great men in history. The first is Hegel's world-historical figure, the man on horseback who consciously and deliberately shapes his world. The second is what used to be known as "a man of providence," someone who perhaps did not intend to play a decisive role but through whom great changes were nonetheless accomplished. Gorbachev was the instrument of change but not the witting shaper of it. He never for a moment envisaged the end of the empire, let alone the end of communism; he came to save and improve the system, not to bury it. One of his harshest critics has said that "he was always a participant in the plot: not the plot that was carried out on August 19 [1991], but the plot that has always existed, which is the plot of the Communist Party against the people, of parasites against their own serfs, of dictators against democracy."[17] That Gorbachev's much-vaunted *perestroika* was recognized to be a hoax in his own land should have been obvious at first sight, for he never succeeded in mobilizing the young people. As Mikhail Heller, the greatest historian of Soviet communism, put it, "History knows of no revolutions that have been carried out by old men alone."[18]

Gorbachev never had an economic program, never had a plan for the nationalities and ethnic groups, and constantly gave contradictory signals on crucial issues. In many cases, he acted as if he were deliberately trying to inflame passions to the utmost, as in the case of Lithuania. The Lithuanians came to him before their vote on independence and asked him what he wanted them to do. They told him that if the vote were held, there would be an overwhelming outpouring of support for independence, and if he did not want that outcome, they would find a way to postpone or cancel the vote. In essence he replied, "You're free to make your own decisions; vote as you wish." When they scheduled the referendum, he gave a speech to the Lithuanians in which he said, "Please don't vote for independence, I may lose my job." When they voted against him, he sent in the Red Army, but without the authority to reestablish Soviet control. Instead, the troops served as a lightning rod, surrounding Radio Vilnius without shutting it down, enraging the population without repressing it, killing a handful of people on their way in, and then pulling in their horns. Gorbachev's actions provoked the maximum possible rage and achieved the minimum possible control.

Gorbachev's actions were so astonishing that I wrote a satirical article in 1986 "exposing" the "fact" that he was a CIA agent, whose mission was to destroy the Soviet system. "I don't know how much we're paying Mikhail Gorbachev," I wrote, "but he's clearly worth every ruble." While my "exposé" was a joke, some of his political enemies in Russia later made the same accusation, and they were certainly not joking. Some news services even called the *American Spectator* to ask whether the claims were serious. Apparently, the idea had occurred to many people, as well it should have. Gorbachev's hollowness was demonstrated once again on his return from being held hostage by the "coup" leaders in August 1991. In his first statement to the nation, Gorbachev said that he still had confidence in the Communist Party as the main instrument of reform. Even as the citadel of communism was being dismantled, Gorbachev called for its remodernization.

It was only a matter of time before Gorbachev was removed—and Soviet communism along with him—because while he might have been a media star in the West, his own people knew a failure when they saw one. Yet, as Andrei Sakharov often said, Gorbachev is very difficult to understand, a most mysterious figure. Can he possibly have believed that there was no longer a nationalities problem in the Soviet Union? Did he really think that the West would continue endlessly to bail out the failed Communist system, provided he made symbolic gestures at reform? Did he, the protégé of Andropov, really believe that communism could be brought back to life?

Strange as it may seem, the answer could be yes. The leaders in the Kremlin often had extremely bad information about some very important subjects. When we finally get a look at the archives of the Soviet Union, we will be surprised at how often and how totally the vaunted intelligence services lied to and otherwise misinformed their superiors. Gorbachev knew that the system was in crisis, but he probably never grasped its depth. He may well have believed that the empire was much more popular than it actually was. Consider for a moment the sort of thing that is being uncovered in the other archives of the fallen empire:

> Digging through Polish Communist Party archives for a study of farm collectivization, Dariusz Jarosz, a 35-year old scholar, realized that he had struck historical gold: a cache of reports by secret-police informers on the mood of ordinary country folk.
>
> "There was no social history allowed in the Communist years," Mr. Jarosz said. "It would have showed that people always rejected Communism." And that, to his delight, is precisely what the records revealed . . . but by the time these initial accounts of social discontent had made their way to the upper echelons of the police bureaucracy, they had been . . . "beautified," Mr. Jarosz said—to land lightly on the eyes and ears of the spies' superiors. Thus was the fiction of a happy Communist society maintained.[19]

The intelligence services misled the top authorities on two of the regime's most important subjects: Andrei Sakharov and the United States of America. In the spring of 1994—long after *glasnost* had come and gone—Sakharov's widow, Elena Bonner, was given sixty-one KGB files on her late husband. She was informed that he had been the most spied-upon Soviet; the archives contained no less than 520 volumes on his human rights activities. "I didn't find anything new," she said after reading the files, "but they upset me, for how the KGB systematically disinformed the country's leaders." The disinformation ran along two lines, first claiming that

Sakharov was actively collaborating with foreign enemies of the Soviet Union to sabotage the Communist system and, second, dramatically understating his popularity among the Russian people. When Sakharov died, the KGB understated the number of mourners by a factor of five. The incredibly misguided information reaching Polish and Soviet leaders from their intelligence services followed a well-known warning: don't bring bad news to Caesar. The political scientists have a more complicated way of describing this phenomenon:

> There is a peculiar and inverse relationship between information and coercion. Systems based on one or the other are completely different. In high coercion systems people only pass on information acceptable to their superiors. The more information of this kind that leaders have, the less they actually know.[20]

The Soviet system was overloaded with bad information, a symptom of its impending death. It could not cope with a world in which information had become all important, because, although the KGB and the Communist Party were quite capable of manipulating information to suit their domestic needs and even deceive the West from time to time, they could not get enough accurate information to remain competitive. Gorbachev's confusion on so many basic issues is perhaps the most eloquent testimony to the system's failure, and the desperation with which he and Shevardnadze begged the West to abolish COCOM and permit the Soviet Union to obtain the West's advanced technology (itself the result of excellent information and analysis) is further confirmation.

In contrast, the peoples of the empire were flooded with accurate information, especially from the enormously important radio broadcasts from the West. Radio Free Europe, Radio Liberty, the Voice of America, the BBC, the German *Deutsche Welle,* and Israel's *Kol Yisrael* reached millions of listeners day after day, providing accurate news, rational analyses, and hope that some day things would change for the better. One of Gorbachev's many mistakes was his failure to recognize the devastating effect of the radio broadcasts, for he proved surprisingly willing to end the jamming of the Western radio broadcasts as part of *glasnost.* In typical schizophrenic fashion, he took sometimes violent action against brave, independent Russian journalists, but the steady flow of information from the West gave the Soviet people a better understanding of the world than the leaders of the empire gave.

The constant flow of bad information to the top of the Soviet pyramid actually put the world on the brink of thermonuclear war. After Reagan took office, the KGB soon came to the conclusion that the United States was preparing to launch a first-strike nuclear attack on the Soviet Union and informed the Kremlin of this "fact." The Red Army went on high alert for several months, and KGB officers in the Washington *residentura* were ordered to watch for such suspicious signs of sinister activity as office lights burning far into the night in the White House, the State Department, and the Pentagon. With this kind of "information"—and remember that as Andropov's political heir, Gorbachev relied heavily on the KGB for his understanding of how the world worked—we should not be surprised at *any* of the nonsense that Soviet leaders believed.

Mikhail Heller, one of the few to recognize the potentially fatal vulnerability of Soviet communism to its growing isolation from the modern world, went a long way in the mid-1980s toward anticipating what was to come:

> In advanced industrial societies, a transition is taking place from an industrial society to one based on information technology. But the Soviet system is incapable of making this transition. Free access to information would lead to its destruction. Yet the Soviet system will have to find ways of adapting to the technological revolution. Otherwise, the Soviet superpower will fall further and further behind militarily and will weaken. The legitimacy of the regime as the "defender" of the country will be seriously shaken and the pride of the once mighty state will be wounded—a pride which for decades has been the people's compensation for the poverty and privations they endured.[21]

Much of what Heller hopefully anticipated did take place. Much information did get through the iron curtain, thanks to the radio broadcasts from the West and the increased openness of the *glasnost* period. The Soviet system did not find effective ways to keep up with the new technology, both because there was not enough money to buy it and because the West—led by Reagan—made a concerted effort to keep it out of Soviet hands. At the end of the day, in keeping with the principles of the Democratic Revolution, it was the people who overthrew Soviet communism. The leaders degenerated into caricatures and were summarily dismissed by Boris Yeltsin, the only national leader with a popular electoral mandate.

Dissident Activity in the Soviet Bloc

As Bukovsky's documents abundantly show, popular hatred of the empire was quite substantial. But it was difficult for the West to see it, primarily of course because most of the dissidents avoided contact with foreigners, knowing the terrible risks such contact entailed. Here and there, however, the signs were present, and it was possible for attentive students, journalists, and even diplomats to notice them. In the summer of 1981, for example, a series of State Department mailgrams (not even cables) arrived in Washington from one of our consular officers in East Germany, who had spent part of his summer vacation traveling around the country and poking his nose into churches. He found clear signs of religious revival, combined with a growing pacifist movement. The reports were purely anecdotal, and, while the State Department's excellent man on the scene was not in a position to judge the breadth or depth of the phenomenon, the very existence of religiously inspired pacifism in the German Democratic Republic was dramatic evidence of the failure of the Communist regime and the profundity of popular opposition to it.

Gorbachev's providential role was to work against his own announced goals and ambitions. His actions encouraged the opponents of communism to take chances, to challenge the old guard, and eventually to sweep the Soviet Empire into the garbage heap of history. That he did not intend any of it does not detract in the least from his extraordinary capacity for creative destruction. At once espousing the legitimacy of protest and demonstrating the impotence of the forces of repression, Gorbachev catalyzed the many elements within the empire that were looking for a chance to escape, destroy, or reform the Communist system. Some of these, like Solidarity in Poland and Charter 77 in Czechoslovakia, were well known; others were more difficult to see. In the late 1970s and early 1980s, for example, dissident Communists from Central and Eastern Europe were meeting once or twice a year to compare notes, discuss strategies, and evaluate the strength of the regimes. These were all members of Communist parties, all nationalists, and all looking for ways to make their countries more independent of Moscow and more democratic. According to the summary of their meeting near Belgrade in late 1981,

> It seems at last possible to see a solution along democratic lines. The situation in all East European countries is now conditioned by events in Poland. . . .
>
> The participants have analyzed the attitude of the USSR as one of weakness in face of the events in Poland. A regime in full control of its means would have never permitted the development of the situation in Poland such as we see it today. This weakness of the USSR constitutes a new fact and must be exploited for the consolidation of the struggle everywhere.[22]

The dissident Communists proceeded to set up Solidarity-type organizations in other East European countries. Needless to say, such coordination was not limited to the Communists. Anti-Communist dissidents throughout the bloc were also meeting to work out joint strategies. As former American ambassador to Czechoslovakia William Luers recalled,

> Almost from the start, the Charter activists were in close, though highly discreet, contact with parallel dissident movements in Hungary and Poland. As early as 1978, Charter leaders conferred secretly with their opposite numbers from Solidarity; with all the clandestine precautions they could muster, they met in the mountain woods on the Polish-Czechoslovak border—not just the first time but repeatedly over the years.[23]

Dissidents against the empire found ways to meet their counterparts throughout the Eastern bloc, and we have only just scratched the surface of the many different ways they met. A Czech organization known as the Jazz Section, for example, started as a unit of the musicians' union and quickly became a political group that "boldly began to engage large numbers of young people in quasi-opposition activities beyond the realm of jazz, which the regime found so distasteful precisely because they understood that

jazz had become a widespread form of protest."[24] In fact, just a
few weeks before the Velvet Revolution broke out, a big jazz con-
cert in Wroclaw, Poland, attracted many thousands of young
Czechoslovaks, hoping to participate in a Central European
Woodstock.

Conclusion

Finally, and inevitably, Gorbachev failed to take the necessary steps
to lock out the greatest threats to the Soviet system. By permitting
John Paul II to travel throughout Poland, giving his insurrection-
ary homilies and inspiring the enemies of communism to challenge that evil, Gorbachev enabled one of his most dangerous and
determined enemies to inspire the peoples of the empire to bring
down communism. The role of the church in Poland was obvious,
but its surprisingly important effect in Czechoslovakia has generally been ignored. As Luers tells us:

> One Civic Forum leader, a philosopher and historian,
> claims to have read in some sixteenth-century Czecho-
> slovak chronicles that Bohemia would achieve indepen-
> dence two weeks after Agnes, the pious Czech princess
> of the thirteenth century, was canonized. In fact, the can-
> onization of St. Agnes was celebrated in St. Vitus' Ca-
> thedral in the Hradcany Castle on November 25, a few
> days before the fall of the communist government. Later
> in the same cathedral during the *Te Deum* celebrating
> Havel's installation as the new president on December
> 29, one of his aides remarked, "St. Agnes had her hand
> under our gentle revolution."[25]

There is no doubt that Pope John Paul recognized the significance of canonizing St. Agnes, for in his homily in Rome on that
occasion, he used the same kind of language as he had in his in-
cendiary talks to the Poles. The pope was using a religious occasion to call for a political change, urging his followers to be brave
in the face of their oppressors and to eschew violence in their fight
for freedom. It was the first canonization of a Czech saint in three
hundred years. Ten thousand Czech and Slovak pilgrims came for
the ceremony in St. Peter's. The next week there was a violent
suppression of a student demonstration in Prague: the Velvet Revo-

lution had broken out. Five months later, the pope was in Prague, meeting with the new Czech leader, Vaclav Havel. As David Willey notes in his book on Pope John Paul II, *The Politician of God,*

> At the time political observers failed to make the connection between the two events, but their significance was immediately clear to the Czech believers: just as in Poland, from the stage of a religious celebration the Pope had helped provide the courage for an audacious political change.[26]

Many men and women contributed to the revolutionary expansion of freedom in the last quarter of the twentieth century, but of that heroic company, John Paul had the most coherent and the broadest vision. It was altogether in keeping with the nature of this extraordinary era that a man of religion, widely criticized by the fashionable intelligentsia as an archreactionary, should actually be the most revolutionary of world leaders.

4

❖

THE REVOLUTION
BETRAYED

By the time the Berlin Wall came down, Ronald Reagan had returned to California, and George Bush had taken up residence in
the White House. As the last American president to have fought in
World War II, Bush might have been expected to have recognized
the defeat of Soviet totalitarianism as at least as significant as the
victory over fascism nearly half a century before. Alas, the spectacular implosion of the Soviet Empire was taken by the Bush administration not so much as cause for celebration and a golden
opportunity to extend democracy as a matter for polite concern.

As the empire came undone, Bush, James Baker, and Brent
Scowcroft scrambled to save Gorbachev. The president himself even
traveled to Ukraine to give what came to be termed the "chicken
Kiev" speech, in which he called on the Ukrainians to abandon
their hopelessly unrealistic dream of independence. Errors of judgment abounded. Even after the old Communists botched their attempt to regain power by putsch, Bush called Yeltsin several times to
urge him to support the Gorbachevian All-Union Treaty, an idea
that had the support of perhaps 3 percent of the Soviet population.

When Gorbachev was rejected by his own people and replaced
by Yeltsin, our leaders did not know what to do: they staggered

from one idea to another, now endorsing massive aid to Russia and the other republics, then dismissing it; now announcing that the old Soviet nuclear weapons were nothing to worry about, then calling for an emergency program to hire Soviet nuclear scientists for fear they would go to work for the rogue states or terrorists. When Richard Nixon warned that Bush might get blamed for "losing Russia," Bush started talking about Russian aid again. Meanwhile, the secretary of state was deepening his friendship with Soviet Foreign Minister Eduard Shevardnadze, an elegant man of impeccable manners who was known to his people as "the butcher of Georgia" for his leadership of the bloody purges during the first half of the 1970s.

The Failures of the Bush Administration

The Fall of Communism. The Bush administration had stumbled during the glorious days of the fall of communism. As he openly admitted, the president and his closest advisers were men and women without much concern for, or intimacy with, the "vision thing." Lacking an understanding of the historic moment, they set themselves the same goal that had guided the "realists" of American foreign policy ever since the cold war began: stability. And to that end, they concentrated their energies on saving the Russian leader, whoever he might be: first it was Gorbachev, later Yeltsin.

Although at times such a style of foreign policy is entirely appropriate, that genteel approach was not well suited to the halcyon days of the late 1980s and early 1990s. We had been fighting for this moment ever since our own revolution, with our major enemy routed, and our own revolutionary values achieving a degree of success never before seen and only rarely imagined. It is given to few generations to live through a moment as profoundly satisfying as the end of communism. We literally watched it die on television, as the pro-Yeltsin forces assaulted the White House in Moscow, from within which the fossilized remnants of the Bolshevik Revolution launched their pathetic cries for insurrection. We should have had an international celebration of democracy and established a worldwide holiday in honor of our great achievement. That we had won the third world war of this century without having to lose the tens of millions of lives sacrificed in the first two should hardly have diminished the magnitude of our victory.

If anything, the triumph of democracy was rendered even more glorious by the fact that it did not need to be achieved through war.

Bush never understood that he was presiding over a moment of exceptional glory for us and our values and that we could stand astride the world like a colossus. At the end of World War II, the vanquished Axis powers and much of the free world looked to America for help, because they were in physical and economic ruin while we were strong and rich. We provided the Marshall Plan to Western Europe (we also offered it to the Soviet Union and its satellites, but Stalin gave orders that it be rejected). We imposed democratic capitalism on West Germany and Japan, purging both governments of those who had been responsible for the crimes of the recent past and helping to educate the next generation in the values and modalities of the free market and democratic politics. In the early 1990s, we were relatively weaker economically (however, this was more than compensated for by the great economic strength of the democratic West) but even stronger politically and militarily. No conceivable enemy could threaten our existence, as had the Soviet Empire after World War II, and the world had no recognizable alternative to our system of democratic capitalism.

With the fall of communism, an era closed, and the world again looked anxiously to Washington for guidance. Most world leaders, assuming that we had a strategic vision for the new era, wanted to align themselves with it as quickly as possible. As religious pilgrims coming to the shrine of their faith, the leaders of the Democratic Revolution came to the American capital to pay homage, to thank us for having made it all possible, and to learn their destinies. The ceremony was quickly ritualized: an address to Congress, expressing gratitude to the American people, and then the trip to the White House to ask what the world's lone superpower had planned for the new era. The procession was an imposing one: from Walesa and Havel to Mandela and Juan Carlos, the heroes of the triumphant war against tyranny passed under our arches and sought guidance from us. But the "vision thing" was not in vogue in those years. Bush and Baker vaguely understood that some deep thoughts were expected of them, and they issued some reassuring words about a New World Order that seemed, oddly, to suggest that the American government hoped the United Nations would somehow figure out what to do. In a word, America had nothing to say.

Our silence should not have been a total shock. The pattern of modern American history is one of brief spasms of international activity, followed by rapid demobilization and prolonged disengagement. After World War I, we unleashed Woodrow Wilson on Europe, calling for the moralization of international affairs and supporting the spiteful Versailles Peace Treaty, and then abruptly reversed course when the Senate decided not to support the League of Nations. After the Wilsonian spasm, we withdrew into righteous solitude, unmoved even by the onslaught of fascism, until the Japanese providentially bombed us into war just in the nick of time. That war won, we determined to bring the boys home and disarm, only to be dragged back into the fray by Stalin's imperialistic ambitions in Europe and Iran and the North Korean invasion of the South.

The Gulf War. The cold war lasted longer than either of the two previous world wars, and we stayed the course for half a century. The cold war won, we were again headed for a dramatic reduction of military power and a minimalist foreign policy, when the Iraqi dictator Saddam Hussein invaded Kuwait, reminding us that the struggle against evil on earth is endless. Saddam provided George Bush with a great opportunity, and up to a point it seemed as if we had once again been saved by our enemies, as Bush mobilized a great army and a great coalition. Backed up by some of the most advanced weapons ever built, he used all the diplomatic tools at his disposal to try to talk the Iraqis out of Kuwait.

The ritual dance that followed between the United States and Iraq was almost biblical. Just as Moses warned Pharaoh that there would be dire consequences if he did not let the Jews go from Egypt, Bush and Baker warned Saddam that if he did not leave Kuwait, a series of terrible plagues would be unleashed upon him. But Saddam ignored the warnings, and so the air war began. At each stage of escalation, he was offered the opportunity to change his mind and end the plagues, but his heart remained hard and one by one the terrible weapons in our arsenal were delivered upon him. His armies were shattered, his cities were destroyed, and his people were killed.

At that point, the biblical analogy breaks down: just as the *coup de grâce* was about to be delivered, while Saddam's airplane awaited him on a Baghdad Tarmac, President Bush, on the advice of his civilian aides and General Colin Powell, the chairman of the Joint Chiefs of Staff, called a sudden and unexpected end to the war, even as he continued to call on the Iraqi people to overthrow the evil regime. The Shiites and Kurds assumed then that the United States would, at a minimum, act to give them a fair shot at winning, but they were deceived. The Bush administration was not about to risk American lives on behalf of the ragtag enemies of Saddam Hussein. The Kurds and the Shiites were crushed, and Saddam lived to fight another day.

Bush and Baker were greatly annoyed by those who criticized the failure of the end game, and in a sense they were entitled to their annoyance. After all, they had been very careful to say that Desert Storm was not aimed at the removal of Saddam; they had called only for the liberation of Kuwait from Iraqi occupation. Had they not kept their word? Why, then, all the criticism? The questions were a bit disingenuous, for most everyone assumed that, while the publicly announced policy was "liberate Kuwait," the *real* policy was "smash Saddam." It seemed preposterous to send half a million men halfway around the world, carrying the most sophisticated weapons ever seen on a battlefield, purely and simply to liberate Kuwait. Because mobilizing so much power for such a meager objective seemed incredible, many assumed that the allies had a more serious, albeit unannounced, goal; and what could it be but the destruction of Saddam Hussein's regime? The removal of Saddam would have served notice on the tyrants of the world that a new world order would prevail, and that the United States would not tolerate gratuitous attacks across recognized international borders. Such an action would also have delivered a most important lesson: no one who challenges the United States will survive in power long enough to brag about it to his children and grandchildren.

More than the logic of the situation led most of the world to assume that Bush and Baker wanted the destruction of Saddam Hussein's murderous regime: it was also the president's words, urging the Iraqi people to rise up. Our refusal to support them was a terrible disgrace, putting us at loggerheads with our own principles and with the great democratic tidal wave that had swept the world. Having led a great global crusade against tyranny, we were now in a position to drive a stake through the heart of a tyrant who had called our bluff. Could anyone have imagined that we would choose such a moment to abruptly call a halt to the operation?

Desert Storm—the actual battle—was a triumph of American power, talent, and will. The end game was a double whammy: Saddam survived, thereby signaling other tyrants that they could challenge the United States and live to fight another day. The Shiites and Kurds were crushed, thereby demonstrating that those who risked their lives for our common cause would not be protected from our common enemies. Permitting Saddam to survive discouraged and demoralized democratic freedom fighters elsewhere. The great triumph of Desert Storm was tragically transformed into the disaster of Desert Shame, for the peoples of the region quite rightly saw the defeat of the Kurds and Shiites as our defeat.

U.S. Policies toward the Former Empire. Desert Shame was of a piece with the Bush-Baker policies toward the fallen Soviet Empire. Although it was clearly in our interest for the empire to disintegrate, not only did we fail to encourage the former satellites to break away and declare their independence, but we were actually quite dismayed when they did so. Just as President Ford refused to meet with Alexander Solzhenitsyn for fear of offending Brezhnev, so Bush was very careful not to upset Gorbachev by giving the slightest support to the likes of Lithuanian leader Landsbergis. When Gorbachev sent troops into Vilnius to assert Soviet imperialist prerogatives in the face of an overwhelming referendum in support of independence, Baker, rather than assert American support for Lithuania's rights—which had been explicitly guaranteed by Gorbachev himself in meetings with the Lithuanian leaders—assured the Kremlin that the United States would impose no economic sanctions.[1] This blind support for Gorbachev went hand in hand with an apparently visceral dislike of his archrival, Boris Yeltsin—whom the Bush White House dismissed early on as unworthy of serious attention. This decision was particularly unfortunate, and not only because Yeltsin won the duel with Gorbachev. Unlike Gorbachev, Yeltsin was elected by the Russian people. Whatever his shortcomings, Yeltsin had democratic legitimacy, and Bush should have understood its importance.

When Yeltsin emerged triumphant following the failed coup in the summer of 1991, we abruptly shifted our personalized policy to support the winner and thereupon repeated the very same mistakes we had made with Gorbachev. Yeltsin's team was nominally committed to democracy and free markets, but they did not have clear ideas about either. Worse still, shortly after the coup, the Russian parliament—of Gorbachev's making—stonewalled all efforts at radical reform, guaranteeing a maddening paralysis that made it impossible to carry out the most fundamental changes, like the wide-scale institution of private property, the creation of a proper legal system to deal with the new political and economic goals, and the creation of orderly methods of oversight and enforcement.

This situation presented us with yet another opportunity to focus on basic principles rather than on personalities. The issue was not whether Yeltsin or some other person was best suited to govern Russia but rather what sort of political and economic system was best. Our two hundred years of experience with a multiethnic society sprawling over an entire continent gave us unique credibility in such matters, and our status as the world's most successful economic system and military power was virtually unchallenged. We should have unhesitatingly provided the Russians—leaders and general public alike—with the lessons we had learned. We should have insisted that the Russians make fundamental structural changes *before* we started pouring money into the reconstruction of the country, since without the structural change the money would simply disappear into a black hole of hopeless undertakings and corrupt operations and organizations.

Furthermore, we should have encouraged Yeltsin to conduct a thorough purge of the system, both in Moscow and in the smaller cities, removing the old Communist *nomenklatura* from its positions of control in all the key institutions of the Russian state and society, particularly the instruments of the Terror. We did not have to limit our efforts to diplomatic channels or personal contacts; we had at our disposal the radio stations that had long lectured the peoples of the Soviet Union on the superiority of democratic capitalism. The radios had been the primary source of reliable information for the most important anti-Communist segments of Russian society. We should have used them to educate the Russian people about the proper functioning of a modern political and economic system and to proclaim the importance of a complete change in the ranks of Russian leadership.

Committed as they were to supporting Russian leaders, Bush and Baker (as later Clinton and Christopher) seem to have thought it possible for the societies of the old empire to pass successfully from communism to democratic capitalism without replacing the bulk of the ruling class. Such a feat was no more possible than it would have been for Germany, Japan, and Italy to pass from fascism to democratic capitalism if we had supported the defeated leaders of those countries and left their followers in key positions. The Nuremberg Tribunal in Germany, the postwar trials in Italy, and MacArthur in Japan made sure that the people of those countries understood the crimes their leaders had committed and that a new era began with a generation of leaders untainted by German nazism, Italian fascism, and Japanese military imperialism. The citizens of the victorious democracies also needed to hear the sory, so that they could better understand the risks they had run and the magnitude of their triumph.

Regimes on Trial. The best way to have told the story would have been to have put the old regimes on trial. The records kept by tyrants could then have documented the people's case against their oppressors. This golden opportunity was missed, in large part because the victorious West declined to proclaim victory and abandoned the Democratic Revolution as quickly as possible. Paradoxically, the great success of the Democratic Revolution made a purge of the defeated tyrants seem less urgent, both because it appeared inevitable that the revolution would sweep them all away without the need for such unpleasantness and because—particularly in the countries of the empire—the evil had contaminated an enormous percentage of the population. Not only would the files contain evidence of crimes from on high, but they would also reveal collaborators throughout the society, "normal" men and women who had been forced to spy and inform and bend to the will of the regime. Citizens of these countries were not eager for all the stories to be told.

Were the peoples of the empire, newly entered upon the road to freedom, prepared to subject themselves to the wrenching trauma of national introspection? It was too much to expect. The initiative, which properly belonged to the victors, could not come from the survivors alone. Yet, unlike the end of World War II, when the victorious armies physically occupied the defeated nations, at the cold war's end the armies of the defeated countries remained intact, indeed untouched. The defeat was political, and if the West were going to demand an accounting from the fallen rulers, it would have to exercise political power to bring it about.

Such an undertaking would have required extraordinary vision and courage. Moreover, it was made even less likely when in those few cases where files were opened to the public—those of the East German Stasi, for example, or the archives of the Czechoslovakian security service—the documents themselves were sometimes found unreliable. Knowing that their careers and perhaps even survival depended on providing their superiors with "information," informants frantically concocted "evidence" even when none truly existed. It was not a question of merely opening the envelope and reading the names of the guilty: one had to check and doublecheck before the truth could be established. In addition, many files were probably altered in the empire's final days by the intelligence services, in anticipation of something like a Nuremberg. The Soviets and their allies would certainly have put us on trial—show trial, to be sure—had they won the cold war and must have expected the same for themselves. Under those circumstances, they destroyed, altered, and falsified all the records they could get their hands on, time and opportunity permitting.

The Soviet Archives. Nonetheless, the West should have insisted on a proper accounting, if not for the millions of collaborators, certainly for the ruling elites. Even if we were not going to insist on punishment of the war criminals, we should have understood the vital importance of making public the historical record of Communist tyranny. Most of that record was in the Soviet archives, especially those of the KGB, the GRU, the Politburo, and the International Department of the Communist Party of the Soviet Union. For a few brief months after the fall of Soviet communism, there was a chance. Boris Yeltsin, who had defeated the Communists in the streets of Moscow and had declared illegal the Communist Party, instructed the director of the Russian archives, Rudolf Pikhoia, to quickly find a way to preserve and make public the Communist Party archives.

After some initial contacts, Pikhoia asked the American Enterprise Institute in Washington, D.C., in early 1992 to take the lead in this project. The two scholars sent by AEI to examine the archives were utterly amazed at what they saw: a huge vault, locked inside an even larger vault, both underground, secure against nuclear attack, and containing the originals (no copies at all) of millions upon millions of documents, from the days of Marx and Engels until the final hours of the party's existence. The vault even contained the political equivalent of a reliquary: items of clothing and personal effects of Marx, Engels, Lenin, Stalin, and the other priests and demigods of the faith. Because a project of this magnitude could not possibly be carried out by a small think tank in Washington, D.C., AEI immediately contacted its counterparts at other scholarly institutions, inviting them to join. Unfortunately, many of them decided the invitation was an opportunity for institutional aggrandizement, and they opened separate negotiations with the Russians, offering profitable joint ventures for blocks of documents.

Had the Russian political scene been more stable, such competition might have been tolerable, and even desirable, allowing the Russians a choice of partners for various pieces of the archives. But in 1992 there was a race against the clock. Within a few months, the Soviet elite, desperate to keep the secrets of the old regime, convinced Yeltsin to issue a decree imposing a "thirty-year rule" on the archives of the Central Committee of the Soviet Communist Party. Thus, we will not see any material later than the early 1960s that has anything to do with "national security," and we will see nothing at all later than 1981. As for the archives of the KGB, the only documents to reach the West are those sold for scalpers' prices to Western news media (and hence somewhat suspect) and those referred to in other archives, such as the Politburo files Vladimir Bukovsky was able to look at, thanks to his personal prestige and prompt action.[2] So long as those archives remain sealed, the Communist jailers, torturers, and murderers who survived the transition will remain entrenched in their old positions of power. The Democratic Revolution will remain unfulfilled, and neither we nor the people of the empire will know the full truth about their leaders' behavior.

Incredibly, no official voice in the West uttered a protest when Boris Yeltsin, after promising to open the Communist archives, summarily issued his secrecy edict. Indeed, some of our most prestigious institutions, like the Hoover Institution and the Library of Congress, were tacit parties to this arrangement since, instead of insisting on open access, they scrambled to outbid one another and made separate deals for older documents. Almost all, in government, journalism, and academe, swallowed the Russians' claim that they were entitled to seal the archives because, after all, they contained "state secrets." Yet the state whose secrets lay in the archives no longer existed, and that defunct state was guilty of some of the most monstrous criminal acts of the century. Was the world not entitled to that information? And did not Yeltsin's concern about secrecy suggest an intention to protect the criminals and even continue some of the criminal practices? No one would have accepted a suppression of evidence of the criminal Nazi, Fascist, and Japanese actions, and there was no reason to do so for the Communists.

Survival of the Communists. With rare exceptions, the Communist leaders were not held accountable for their crimes, and most of the *nomenklatura* managed to survive in place. The "post-Communist" Russian Duma remained at the mercy of an antidemocratic bloc of "former" Communists. The state bureaucracy remained in the hands of the same people who had wrecked the country by designing and administering the catastrophic five-year plans of the *ancien régime*. Even the bulk of the KGB remained in place; after a brief period with the democratic leadership of Vadim Bakatin, Russian intelligence returned to the control of top officials from the Communist past. As Bakatin put it in an interview:

> Everyone says that Bakatin has torn down the KGB structure. For goodness' sake, this is not so . . . not a single hair has fallen from the head of any official in Kazakhstan. Or to Kyrgyzstan—I just got back from there, everything is still as it was there. The situation is the same in the Moscow department, and in the Kemerevo one. That is, all the capillaries at the bottom and the structures have remained the same.[3]

To be sure, Yeltsin was not the protégé of Andropov, as Gorbachev had been, and he gave less political weight to the secret intelligence service than his predecessor had. But a democratic society could not come into being so long as the old structures of the KGB remained basically intact. With the passage of time, the new Russian intelligence organization—the SVR—forged the same intimate relationships with its counterparts in neighboring republics as the KGB had in the past. In most cases, the people involved were the same as before. Of all the ex-satellites, only Bulgaria purged the former spies from its diplomatic service; the rest remained in place. By mid-1995, the head of British Intelligence told Parliament that Russian spying on the West remained at a very high level, roughly equal to that before the fall of communism. Perhaps the most reliable indicator of the continuity of the KGB's power is that, despite dozens of defections from the Soviet and other bloc intelligence services to the West, no officers at the highest rank—colonels or generals—passed to the other side.[4] And by early 1996, the former head of the First Chief Directorate of the KGB, comrade Yevgeni Primakov, had been named Russian foreign minister. The Communist elite had survived.

Bush and Baker anticipated the error of "Desert Shame": once the enemy forces were routed, the Americans had no inclination to finish the job. Just as Saddam Hussein survived to fight another day, so the communist *nomenklatura* was permitted to endure, thereby thwarting the best chance for a rapid and profound democratic transformation of the Soviet Union and the former satellites. This issue was not simply a question of politics; if the Soviet state were to be dismantled and the state-owned "enterprises" given into private hands, it was difficult to imagine this change being effectively accomplished by the administrators of "real socialism."

Efforts to Settle Accounts. Of course, a few, even in the new democracies, clamored for a settling of accounts with their former oppressors. By and large, though, the new leaders called for a binding up of their nations' wounds so that they could get on with the important mission of building a new society. Men of undoubted anti-Communist credentials like Havel and Walesa argued against Nuremberg-type trials, and even efforts such as the Germans' attempt to put East German tyrant Erich Honneker on the stand came to naught. Only the Czech Republic adopted laws barring former high-ranking Communists from top government jobs, and even this moderate "lustration" policy was highly controversial.

Yet without a settling of accounts, and the elimination of the *nomenklatura*, it was hard to imagine a clean break with the past. Unless the citizens of the new democracies understood in detail what had happened during the Communist era, they would be open to the temptation of returning the old guard to political power when and if things got tough in the near future. If they did not know chapter and verse about the *nomenklatura* of the old regime, how could they vote intelligently? Because many of the candidates came from the crowd that wrecked the countries, it was important to distinguish the real Communists from those who had had little choice in political or economic affairs. For the truly guilty to recycle themselves without penalty would be a terrible tragedy; yet without making public the grim chapters and verses sitting in the archives, liars and criminal scoundrels were bound to flourish.

As in 1945, America had won an ideological war, and the victory had demonstrated the superiority of American ideals and society. Bush had fought in World War II, had witnessed the purge of Fascists in Europe and warlords in Japan, and had seen the triumph of democracy in those countries once they had been rid of those who had led them into evil and defeat. Bush should have remembered the lessons of the war, but he did not. Instead, he took the soft option: credits for Gorbachev, credits for Yeltsin. Clinton followed in Bush's footsteps, and in time we found ourselves in the absurd position of endorsing a "war crimes tribunal" for Serbs but dealing with the mass murderers of the Soviet epoch as if they were entitled to respect, even honor. If it was right to call Milosevic to account for the ethnic cleansing in Bosnia, why not Gorbachev and Shevardnadze for the torture and murders in Russia, Georgia, and Afghanistan? Was the Serbian campaign in Bosnia any bloodier than the Soviet war in Afghanistan?

The Role of Russia in Europe. In like manner, Bush failed to address the central question of the new European order: what sort of role would Russia now play? The Central Europeans, above all, appealed to NATO to extend its security umbrella right up to the Russian frontier, guaranteeing Poland, Czechoslovakia, and Hungary, at a minimum, against future Russian imperialism. The Russians wailed that this expansion of NATO would constitute undue interference in their legitimate interests and would even threaten their own security. But this posture should not have been taken seriously. Was the West not entitled to assert, as the pope had argued in the last decade of the cold war, that the Yalta line—and hence the Soviet occupation of Eastern Europe—was illegitimate? And was the United States not entitled to reassert the time-honored principle of self-determination of nations? To back down in the face of Russian growls was only to undermine further the confidence of the world in American leadership. But the "vision thing" was not in vogue in the White House.

Controlling Sensitive Technology

So eager were the Americans to "help Yeltsin" that they rapidly undid one of the keystones of Reagan's successful policies. Acting on information from the KGB provided by agent Farewell, the Reagan administration had managed to strangle the pipeline to the Soviet Union of militarily useful advanced technology. Export controls were tightened, new enforcement mechanisms were put in place, and thousands of U.S. and allied customs agents were put to work to discover, block, or at least track exports of militarily useful technology. The core of this vast international network was COCOM, originally a NATO committee to manage the economic embargo against the Soviet bloc that later became a sleepy bureaucratic outpost housed in an annex of the U.S. Embassy in Paris. After the Pentagon gave new clout to COCOM, it was the true international hub of American-led export controls by the mid-1980s, involving all NATO countries except Iceland, as well as Japan and Australia. The Reagan policy worked.

Bush, Baker, and Scowcroft, however, yielded to repeated pleas from Gorbachev and Shevardnadze, who begged the West to abolish COCOM and treat the Soviet Union like any other "normal country." The U.S. military was instructed to prepare a "core list" of very important military technology it would dread seeing in the world's arms bazaar. The Joint Chiefs of Staff committed an act of tragic folly, recommending decontrol of such vital technologies as advanced underwater equipment, special grinders and diamond turning machines (which could be used to manufacture laser mirrors and small nuclear weapons), specialized digital displays for mapping, satellite imagery and image analysis (with no upper limit on performance), and specialized microprocessors and advanced semiconductor manufacturing technology. This last act of largess gave the Russians the ability to produce microelectronics more advanced than those deployed by American forces in the Gulf War. In a single stroke, thanks entirely to the foolishness of the American military leadership and the Bush administration, the Russian Army gained ten years in development and deployment time.

At the same time, the Bush administration decontrolled advanced digital computers, far more powerful than those targeted by the KGB just a few years earlier, including "ruggedized" computers suitable for use on the battlefield (a technology the Russians did not possess, and, like so much of the technology decontrolled by Bush and later by Clinton, unavailable from non-American sources). These massive decontrols enabled the Russians to leapfrog years ahead and to send better weapons to such clients as Iraq, Libya, and Syria.

Clinton—The Counterrevolution

While George Bush did not understand the imperatives of the Democratic Revolution and failed to grasp his historic moment, Bill Clinton was a counterrevolutionary. A primal scream against excessive state power, from the military dictatorships of Franco and Salazar at the beginning, to the Latin American *caudillos*, the Communist Quislings of Central Europe, the Baltics and the Central Asian puppet Socialist republics, and finally the Soviet Empire itself, the Democratic Revolution was an expression of self-confidence by peoples everywhere, who believed that they were mature enough to take back from the state a substantial degree of control over their own destinies.

While our focus is naturally drawn to the dramatic examples of fallen tyrannies, the Democratic Revolution had a substantial effect on our own side of the Yalta line: by the time Clinton was elected, virtually every welfare state in the West had embarked on a mission to dismantle the failed system. State-owned businesses were privatized in France, England, Spain, Italy, Germany, Portugal, and India and even in the Socialist heartland of Scandinavia. This trend, too, was part of the triumph of our ideals, for the West Europeans saw that the collectivist enterprise had failed, while our model of freer markets and maximum individual liberty was, with all its faults, far more successful.

Clinton's Vision. During the presidential campaign, Clinton sounded as if he understood the revolution and often embraced its central themes: reduce the weight of the state, cut the bureaucracy down to size, give more power to state and local governments and, ultimately, to the people themselves. But this illusion quickly shattered. Like so many of his generation, Clinton was steeped in the ideals of academic socialism at Marx-fixated universities. Once in office, Clinton reverted to the language of the statist, repackaging the words much ridiculed by Ronald Reagan as "the scariest sentence in the English language: 'Hello, I'm from the Government and I'm here to help you.'" Clinton spoke of "reinventing government" and "establishing a new partnership between government and business." These became code words for more government, more control from the top, and less freedom for the individual citizen—while deceptively implying the opposite. It was the latest version of the language of 1960s-style democratic socialism, long the ideal of the liberal elite in the United States, and it flew in the face of a decade and a half of global revolution.

The prime symbol of Clinton's counterrevolutionary vision was the health care policy debate, during which Clinton proposed to create an entirely new welfare-state bureaucracy along the lines of the systems already in place in Canada and most of Western Europe. Little notice was taken of the breakdown of that very system in Europe or that even Germany, the wealthiest of the welfare states, was forced to cut back on its health care provisions because not even it could afford the expense. Clinton, paying no heed to these lessons, plowed ahead as if Sweden or the German Federal Republic were a model for the future rather than a failed experiment. The revolutionary imperative was "power to the people," but Clinton's policies concentrated more power in the hands of the *nomenklatura.*

The same pattern held in foreign policy. The revolutionary imperative was to assist democratic forces, but from the first minutes of his presidency, Clinton showed no interest whatsoever in advancing the cause of the Democratic Revolution. In addition, he demonstrated a remarkable ignorance of the way the world works. Having based his career on a willingness to say almost anything that his audience—political, sexual, academic, or legal, as the case may be—found appealing, he was shocked to learn that the rest of the world took his utterances seriously. When his loose remarks before the inaugural about opening the gates to Haitian refugees inspired tens of thousands of Haitians to prepare for a desperate rush across the open sea toward our shores, Clinton had to backpedal to prevent a major loss of life. This pattern has held for the Clinton presidency, in which policies are announced, only to be drastically changed within days or even hours.

Clinton's Intentions. Candidate Clinton ran from the Right against Bush's foreign policy, accusing him of excessive timidity over Bosnia, selling lethal weapons to Saddam, and being soft on the Chinese Communists. It was all true, but Clinton lied about his own intentions. Although Bush was unduly attentive to the Chinese—lobbying Congress to continue most-favored-nation status—Clinton has far outdone him.

He has, for example, rewarded the Chinese for their murderous repression by selling them even more weapons and advanced technology and by sending Mrs. Clinton to Beijing to put a stamp of American approval on the regime. Bush blindly supported Gorbachev, even when the Russian people had voted enthusiastically against him; and Clinton, guided by the longtime Gorbachev acolyte Strobe Talbott, advanced "don't annoy Yeltsin" as the first principle of his European policy, even as it became obvious that Yeltsin was not up to the challenge.

Clinton properly lambasted Bush for weakening our control over advanced technology, thereby enabling Saddam Hussein to strengthen his arsenal, but Clinton went even further, virtually dismantling the entire structure of export controls. This president, a Democrat, adopted policies that have traditionally been associated with big-business Republicans. The best example is the shocking decontrol of powerful computers.

Decontrol of Computers. The government measures computers in terms of CTPs (composite theoretical performance), expressed in MTOPS (millions of theoretical operations per second). The popular 486 personal computer, for example, is 12.5 MTOPS, which was the decontrol level until 1992. Anything from 200 on up was considered a supercomputer. In 1992, the Bush administration had asked COCOM to raise the decontrol level to 25, but COCOM had rejected the request, in part because some of the members thought it was too dangerous and in part because they saw it as a move by the United States to capture the market for its own companies. Bush, unmoved, unilaterally raised the CTP decontrol level to 25, to the unconcealed fury of other COCOM members.

At the outset of the Clinton administration, the computer companies had asked that the decontrol level be raised to 110, which would make available to any buyer highly advanced work stations with CAD/CAM or signal-processing capabilities superior to anything then in use in the U.S. defense sector. With such powerful computers, a country like Iraq could design and "test" ballistic or cruise missiles until an actual flying prototype was available. Unless we had somebody able to report to us on the activities at secret Iraqi work stations, we would have no clue about their operations. Worse still, since computers can be expanded rather easily (much as we might add memory chips to our personal computers), there would be a magnifier effect on the decontrol.

Clinton announced his first decontrol in September 1993: nearly twice the industry's request, in addition to a promise to ask COCOM to raise the level to 500. Our allies were enraged, and not a single other COCOM member approved the American position. Clinton backed down to his fallback position, the original industry request, but it was only a tactical retreat. The second announcement came at the end of March 1994: decontrol through 1,000 MTOPS (except for sales to North Korea). In the meantime, COCOM had quietly expired. The member countries, although unable to agree on the details, nonetheless had agreed it was urgent to control the proliferation of technologies of mass destruction, and all promised they would observe the restrictions of the COCOM control list until a new set of rules could be defined.

Within minutes of COCOM's death, Clinton betrayed his own pledge by unilaterally decontrolling roughly two-thirds of the list and creating a special category for the People's Republic of China that specifically decontrolled the bulk of advanced technology for sale to that country. And yet, in one of those wildly misleading announcements that have come to characterize the Clinton administration, the Commerce Department's Bureau of Export Administration claimed that "current [COCOM] control lists will be retained by the member nations until a successor regime is established." The real story came several paragraphs farther down: "all licensing [is] subject to national discretion," which, in Clinton's case, means anything goes.

The computers were decontrolled with full knowledge that the Chinese would use them in some very sensitive areas. As early as October 1993, Secretary of Defense William Perry announced in Beijing that he had told the Chinese they could cut back on their nuclear testing by using advanced computers to simulate the explosions, adding that the United States was prepared to share this know-how. The simulations required advanced supercomputers, still restricted for sale to the PRC, but this problem was quickly solved by Clinton's massive decontrol of computers. While it is true that the computer simulations might reduce the need for some nuclear testing, it also permits the Chinese to conduct their nuclear program with greater secrecy, thereby making it far more difficult for the West to find out what the PRC is up to in this most delicate area.

Military Technology and the Appeasement of China. The computer sales are only the tip of a very large and ominous iceberg. A recent story involving the aircraft company, McDonnell Douglas, shows the eagerness with which Clinton has provided the Chinese with valuable military technology. Led to believe it could cash in on a 1993 Chinese proposal to purchase large numbers of civilian aircraft (a good part of which would be coproduced in China) and pledged to eliminate a billion dollars of corporate debt, McDonnell, in violation of export-control legislation, permitted the Chinese to visit a plant in Columbus, Ohio, where parts for the B-1 bomber and the C17 strategic transport were manufactured. The Chinese took extensive notes, photographs, and even videotapes, involving advanced five-axis machinery used to manufacture some of the key components of the strategic aircraft, as well as for cruise missiles and nuclear warheads.

Workers at the plant, already enraged by McDonnell's decision to phase out the facility, protested against the Chinese inspection tours. To avoid the workers' wrath, McDonnell smuggled the Chinese in at night or on weekends. The Chinese were so keen to get their hands on the technology that they linked future cooperation with McDonnell to their ability to buy the machinery (a top executive of the Chinese purchasing company wrote the president of Douglas Aircraft that the success of the proposed purchase "shall have a big influence on . . . long-term cooperation").

Even though other American companies were interested in buying the equipment, McDonnell, enticed by Chinese promises to buy dozens of jointly produced MD-90 passenger planes (the latest version of the DC-9), asked for permission to sell it to the PRC at bargain basement prices (about ten cents on the dollar). The Commerce Department approved an export license in September 1994. The contents of the factory filled 280 semitrailers, which were driven to the West Coast, whence the stuff was shipped to China. In essence, a modern American defense plant was simply broken down and shipped to the PRC.

Only an administration hellbent on selling anything and everything to the PRC would have approved the sale, for the international agreements among the Nuclear Suppliers Group forbids selling five-axis machinery to any country known to be a nuclear "proliferator," and the PRC is defined as a "proliferation concern" by the United States itself. To justify this extraordinary action, the licenses stipulated that the five-axis machines would be sent exclusively to a new Chinese facility in Beijing, where they could be monitored. But that facility did not exist. The Chinese had created a Potemkin factory to acquire the technology, which was destined for military facilities. Those in the intelligence community expected this sort of sleight of hand to happen (and they could have deduced it from the public record: similar joint ventures with Boeing were already up and running without such advanced machinery). In the event, six of the machines were illegally diverted to Nanchang, a major center for Chinese missile programs.

By the spring of 1995, McDonnell realized it had been duped. The machines had gone to a military facility, and the Beijing factory was a hoax. McDonnell prudently informed Commerce of the Chinese diversion and asked that the license be suspended. Commerce did that and began an investigation. But before its completion, the Chinese came up with another scheme: why not send the machines to a factory in Shanghai that was already part of the joint venture with McDonnell? McDonnell filed a request to amend the export license, and Commerce approved it without waiting for the final results of the investigation into the diversion. It is hard to imagine a more classic act of appeasement: a sale that never should have been approved in the first place turns out to have been an illegal diversion, but instead of punishing the criminals involved, the Clinton administration simply covered it up by rewriting the documents.

As if this were not enough, it turned out that McDonnell was hotly pursuing another project with the Chinese, which would expand its MD-90 facility at Shenyang to manufacture parts for a smaller version, the MD-95. Some officials in the Defense Department were concerned that advanced machine tools at Shenyang were grossly underutilized, and they soon found an explanation. On February 5, 1996, a joint Chinese-Russian project was announced for the construction of Su-27 fighters—one of the most advanced in the world—at Shenyang. No clearer proof could be imagined of the military value of the McDonnell hardware. One would hope our president would come down hard on a company that was contributing so mightily to Chinese military power, but instead, at a campaign-style appearance at McDonnell in California on February 23, Clinton announced that the government was buying another batch of McDonnell military transports.

Clinton and his administration do not seem worried by anything the Chinese might care to do. The *Washington Times* revealed on February 5 that the intelligence community had discovered that China was shipping the Pakistanis components for their nuclear weapons program. This leak, nicely timed to coincide with the Washington visit of China's foreign minister, shamed the administration into promising to raise the issue with the minister. Another leak—this time that the Chinese are providing Iran with the technology for advanced chemical weapons factories—appeared just in time for the arrival in Washington of Iran's national security adviser. But why should the Chinese worry? Clinton had decontrolled the supercomputers and pointedly refused to take punitive action when advanced technology was illegally diverted to military projects.

The Clinton administration's threats to "get tough" with the PRC (Mickey Kantor's threatening sanctions against Chinese pirating of CDs, videos, and software and William Perry's asking the Chinese to mind their manners on human rights and weapons exports) are only words, and the words are belied by its actions. Just before the release of the State Department's criticism of Chinese human rights practices in the spring of 1995, the White House announced the lifting of yet another sanction on the PRC: American companies like Loral, Hughes, and Lockheed Martin could use Chinese rockets to put their satellites into orbit. It does not take a Confucian scholar to understand the meaning of Clinton's behavior: the words assuage his domestic critics, but the actions strengthen and delight the Chinese.

Threats to U.S. Security. Down this road of folly, great tragedies await us and our allies. In the spring of 1996, Admiral Scott Redd, commander of U.S. naval forces in the Persian Gulf, expressed alarm about China's shipment to Iran of C-801 and C-802 antiship cruise missiles. Secretary Perry's spokesman, Ken Bacon (formerly of the *Wall Street Journal*), immediately told the press that the missiles were "no threat" to the Navy. It is no mere semantic issue, for if the Chinese missiles do in fact threaten our ships—as Admiral Redd believes—the State Department must invoke sanctions against the PRC, as required by the 1992 Defense Authorization Act. Whom should we believe, the person risking life and limb on the deck or the bureaucrats in Washington trying to put a good face on Clinton's appeasement of the PRC?

Any doubts about the Clinton administration's nonchalant attitude toward Chinese military power should have been resolved by an interview Clinton gave to *New York Times* columnist Thomas Friedman. In that interview, Clinton revealed that he had told Chinese President Jian Zemin that America's greatest "national security" concern about China was "that all of your people will want to get rich in exactly the same way we got rich. And unless we try to triple the automobile mileage and to reduce greenhouse gas emissions, if you all get rich in that way we did, we won't be breathing very well." Clinton made this amazing confession a few short weeks after the Chinese had carried out an attempt at military intimidation of Taiwan, on the occasion of the first democratic election of a Chinese national leader in five thousand years.

And where were the Republicans on these vital questions? Obsessed with the budget and oblivious to national security, they made hardly a peep as some of our finest technology—supposedly our competitive edge against both military and economic adversaries—was laid into the hands of a regime totally hostile to our values and then used to assist some of our worst enemies. If Clinton was criminally irresponsible by directly strengthening the world's last major Communist dictatorship and indirectly aiding China's terrorist friends and nuclear wannabees in the Middle East, Congress and the presidential candidates were accessories to the fact.

Clinton's China policy is often rationalized by the theory that we can best influence the behavior of the PRC by enmeshing it in a vast network of trade and credits. Clinton has insisted on most-favored-nation status to China, even though the Chinese are in blatant violation of our human rights standards and are known to be shipping dangerous weapons to such international malefactors as Iran and North Korea. Trade with China, no matter how dangerous the technology sold to Beijing, is hailed as the lucrative solvent that will dissolve the unpleasant PRC policies. The late secretary of commerce, Ron Brown, often bragged about a new relationship that would enrich both countries. For those old enough to remember, this theory was tested in the mid-1970s on the Soviet Union, when Richard Nixon and Henry Kissinger called it "détente." It did not change Soviet behavior: instead, it made the Soviets technologically and militarily more powerful. It will certainly do the same for the Chinese.

Finally, driving the last nail into the lid of antiproliferation's coffin, Clinton terminated reexport controls. Now, there is no longer any way to ensure that clients of ours will not sell our technology to our enemies. Even as Clinton issued stern warnings to North Korea, Iran, and Iraq, he destroyed our best hope of keeping their murderous hands off the most dangerous technology in the world.

The Foreign Policy Mess. Getting to the root cause of the foreign policy mess is difficult, because understanding how the process worked is almost impossible. The various cabinet secretaries have often made conflicting statements on basic policy issues—our willingness to use force, for example, and our intentions toward rogue countries like North Korea. Such contradictions are not supposed to happen *ever*; in the Clinton administration they have happened regularly. As a result, we have not known who spoke for the administration, and neither have our allies and enemies. On too many occasions when tough talk has come from the administration, no sustained action backed it up. For nearly three years, in the face of the catastrophe in Bosnia, for example, we would bomb for a few minutes and then go away. As a result, our allies have diminished confidence in us, and our enemies have no respect for us or fear of us—as proved by the Serbs' confident advance on Bosnia until the autumn of 1995.

Bosnia was the Clinton administration's first challenge. His campaign rhetoric—that Bush had been too craven and had forsaken the former Yugoslavia—still rang in our ears. Yet when Warren Christopher went to Europe in May 1993 with the announced intention to convince our NATO allies to lift the arms embargo on Bosnia (so the Bosnians could defend themselves against the Serb invasion of their territory) and to commit American air power to meaningful airstrikes against Serb forces, the

Europeans were not enthusiastic. So Christopher—with Clinton's approval—abandoned his policy within a few days.

When Clinton was finally shamed into committing greater military power against the Serbs—and this only after the Croatians decided to carve out their own colonial area in poor Bosnia—he drew the wrong conclusions. After several days of pummeling from American air power, the Serbs sued for peace, came to Dayton, Ohio, and agreed to terms. No American or allied ground forces had been necessary to bring about this most welcome armistice. Yet instead of recognizing that air power—like the sword of Damocles—could be effectively wielded as the ultimate "peace-keeper," Clinton surprisingly concluded that tens of thousands of allied troops should be sent for that purpose, thereby offering a huge number of targets and potential hostages to those who wanted to scuttle the peace.

This sort of perennial confusion is only to be expected from a president who has paid little attention to diplomacy and conflict. Even a casual perusal of President Clinton's daily calendars shows that he has been uniquely disengaged from foreign policy. Most modern presidents insisted on daily intelligence briefings first thing in the morning, but Clinton's working day has started quite late, with a big block of "private time" lasting until 10 or even 11 o'clock. Personal briefings from the director of central intelligence, a staple for most recent presidents, have been exceedingly rare. Even meetings with the national security adviser—his own foreign policy manager—have been far less frequent than in previous administrations. It might be thought that this offhanded approach to international affairs was simply a personal eccentricity of Bill Clinton's, but in fact it was a deliberate, reasoned decision taken at the cabinet level:

> It is evidently a point of pride . . . that the United States has no central strategy, no global vision, no geopolitical concept to guide its actions. . . . Addressing a closed door meeting of State Department personnel in Washington soon after taking office, Christopher . . . responded to a question about America's strategy for the post Cold War world by declaring that we neither had nor needed any such thing. . . . He went on to explain that it would be American policy to respond on a "case-by-case" basis to contingencies . . . an approach he said

he had adopted with good results in the practice of corporate law.[5]

The Clinton administration's first impulse was to reject the notion that America has any special role to play in the world: there has been no American strategy. Clinton had no inclination that America should lead; like Bush, he preferred that the United States not act by itself but coordinate with others. He was therefore comfortable with running our policies through NATO or the United Nations, and if the Europeans or Boutros Boutros-Ghali could not decide on a common policy, Clinton was content to do nothing. American action thus required international approval.

Clinton's lack of understanding of the world and our unique role in it left him without a proper yardstick with which to measure the issues he had to decide. Our policy in the former satellite countries should have been to encourage a very rapid transition to democratic capitalism, making our wealth and our expertise available to those who worked in that direction. But Clinton seems never to have grappled with this question. American aid flowed into Russia without interruption, regardless of the twists and turns of official policy in the Kremlin. Clinton's Russia policy—the second "impulse"—was a simple replay of the failed Bush policy, resting on blind, unconditional support for the Russian leader. Clinton gave Yeltsin almost everything he wanted and rarely, if ever, asked for anything meaningful in return.

In 1995, when the Red Army staggered into Chechnya, Secretary of State Christopher immediately proclaimed it a "Russian internal problem," as if we, and our European allies, had no reason to worry about Russian armed forces moving across national borders. And throughout the first three years of the Bosnia crisis, Clinton was extremely deferential to Yeltsin's desire to play a major role. But since Yeltsin generally took a pro-Serbian position, and since it was obvious to any impartial observer that the Serbs had invaded Bosnia without justification, accommodating Yeltsin meant a further sacrifice of the Bosnians. Only after the Serbs had demonstrated their contempt for Western warnings by continuing to bomb Sarajevo—where television cameras could instantly relay the scenes of horror to mass audiences in Western countries—did anything more than token reprisals occur.

Meanwhile, on the important question of expanding NATO to include the new democracies of Hungary, the Czech Republic, and Poland, Clinton beat a quick retreat after some early bravado, proposing instead a vague "Partnership for Peace" that convinced the Central Europeans only that enhanced security for them would never come from this administration. The greatest threat to their security is an expansionist Russia, but Clinton was not prepared to grapple with *that* one.

The third Clintonian impulse is a kind of pidgin mercantilism. Clinton has sometimes acted as if he believed that the most important thing he could do in the world was increase American exports. He took extraordinary actions to free up advanced computers for export and made various raucous sorties against Japanese import duties on American products. He has fought tenaciously to maintain most-favored-nation status for the PRC. The unfortunate campaign slogan, "It's the economy, stupid!" has been applied to foreign policy as well.

While no one can argue against encouraging American exports—although whether the best method is direct lobbying by the president and his cabinet secretaries is doubtful—exports cannot possibly form the core of a coherent American foreign policy. The long-term effect of this kind of trade-for-its-own-sake is to ensure that we will face fierce commercial competition in areas where we could easily maintain an overwhelming domination. Such a policy also ensures that the American fighting men and women of the future will face our own best technology on hostile battlefields. Clinton sold the Chinese superb American technology for advanced weapons systems, which they then resold to rogue nations like Libya, Iran, North Korea, and Syria. Because America is inevitably drawn into conflict with dictatorships, we should maintain the greatest possible strategic advantage over all such countries.

The overemphasis on trade has also led to a touching faith in the power of embargoes. These have sometimes been effective but have more often failed to achieve any political objective other than providing a warm moral glow for the embargoers. Too often, embargoes are ineffectual exercises in international showmanship. After Russia and China, we have no more vexing question for our national interest than Iran, but our policy under Clinton has consisted almost entirely of a fatuous unilateral embargo. The net effect of this policy was to transfer lucrative contracts from American firms to European and Asian competitors. At the same time,

Clinton has long refused to lift the one really effective (because multilateral) embargo in which we participated: the arms embargo against the poor Bosnians. We have good reason to believe he wanted to lift the embargo on Cuba, but the potential political fallout was too great. Nonetheless, he did take steps to appease Castro, agreeing that future refugees would be sent back to the island. We withheld help from those we ostensibly wanted to help and cut a shameful deal with the only Communist dictator in our hemisphere.

Finally, Clinton has a visceral distrust and dislike of the military. His first actions in office concerned the treatment of homosexuals in the armed services. After the initial political turmoil following his off-the-cuff remark that he favored an end to the ban, Clinton promised the chiefs of staff that he would not take action without careful coordination with them. He nonetheless proceeded to announce a new policy without such coordination, thereby opening a rift that was never healed. The point here is not the issue of gays in the military but the very important relationship between commander in chief and America's military establishment. The combination of a president in whose word the military forces have no confidence, a constantly shifting mélange of policies and reactions, the image of a Clinton who avoided military service himself, and the drastic reduction of the military budget was damaging to the morale and the strength of our armed forces.

To be sure, it would have taken an unusually farsighted and tough-minded president to buck a global tide against military spending: as always at the end of a war, public opinion throughout the Western democracies turned briskly in favor of slashing defense expenditures, and the status of the armed forces dropped dramatically. Bush did not hesitate to jump on this bandwagon. Had it not been for Saddam Hussein, the military would have suffered deeper cuts. Clinton just increased the tempo. Both George Bush and Bill Clinton mouthed the newly conventional wisdom that, in the post–cold war world, it would be economic strength, not military might, that would determine a country's standing. Such "wisdom" is cold comfort indeed to the Bosnians, the Chechnians, and the hundreds of thousands of African widows and orphans.

The 1994 Elections and the Power of Revolutionary Values. The pollsters and the political scientists insist that American elections are won and lost in the pocketbook, not in the global arena. I believe, however, that Bill Clinton's thrashing at the hands of the American electorate in 1994 was at least in good part a response to his betrayal of the Democratic Revolution, at home and abroad. Clinton was one of the few world leaders who still believed in central planning, and the American people wanted none of it.

No economic "factors" could explain the stunning defeat of Democratic candidates in November 1994. Not a single Republican incumbent was defeated in the hundreds of elections for House and Senate seats; the overwhelming majority of Republicans won at the state and local levels as well. The American people were in an ideological rage against a president who had misled them in his own campaign and turned his back on the American mission. In that act of creative destruction, the American people rejoined the Democratic Revolution.

The single message that runs from Moscow to Mexico and from Warsaw to Washington is that the people believe in themselves. Having lived through a century of tyranny, in which even the most libertarian countries expanded their governments and limited the freedom of their citizens, we are ready to resume the great democratic experiment.

The people have a clear vision of the kind of political system they want: they want less. They want institutions over which they can exercise greater control: smaller, leaner, more responsive, more efficient, and less expensive institutions. They do not believe that the politicians or the intellectuals are better decision makers than they are, and so they see no reason to give more and more money to government. These demands are an integral part of the revolutionary movement for greater individual freedom and political democracy, and its slogans go back to the origins of the American Republic: "Taxation without representation is treason" is as true when applied to the contemporary Washington bureaucracy as it was when directed at George III.

Just as those words were a revolutionary call for democratic self-government (and not just a "taxpayers' revolt") in the eighteenth century, so they are today, for they are aimed at the power of the state over its citizens. Both Reagan and Thatcher rode these themes to power and used them to inspire millions around the world. That neither leader fully succeeded in convincing the political classes of England and the United States to diminish their own power voluntarily is testimony to how much remains to be done. Yet we must be indebted to Reagan and Thatcher for having understood that freedom is indivisible: the democracies must fight for it both at home and abroad. If the West introspectively addresses its own problems without supporting like-minded people elsewhere, the freedoms achieved at home will inevitably be threatened by the success of tyrants abroad.

The established classes and their allies in the academy and the media are attempting to explain away the revolutionary impulse by claiming that it is a protest by a narrow segment of the population (angry white males, for example) against a particular set of policies or politicians, or against the reek of corruption, and not a call for freedom from excessive government as such. Desperate to maintain their power and their privileges, they constantly seek to capture the revolutionary movement by a call for "reform." But their so-called reforms are merely more government power. Instead of smaller government and more freedom and democracy, they propose ever more and ever larger units and new governing bureaucracies. Whether calling for a "new Europe," run by the governmental professionals in Brussels and Bonn, or a "Confederation of Independent States" led by Moscow, or a "New World Order," centered on UN headquarters in New York, or a "new partnership between government and business," as Clinton described his own plans for the expansion of Washington's role in the private sector, they offer only bigger misgovernment-as-usual.

Yet the established classes are like little Canutes, ordering the waves to retreat, and their seawalls are crumbling before our eyes. The symbol of the "new Europe"—the single currency—has been deferred far into the future. The Maastricht chorus, which was to have been the prelude to a new European symphony, seems more likely to have been the swan song of the old order. In America, Bill Clinton's call to imitate the failed health policies of the European welfare state catalyzed a violent backlash against the very idea of any further expansion of the state.

The people yearn for the real thing: revolution, the whole nine yards. They want government to be slashed down to size, so that power can be returned to its source. The people have expressed it in the best way available to them, by telling their politicians, in government and out, to go to hell. Is this not the message of the post–cold war years? The great garbage bin of history is stuffed with fallen leaders and their parties and movements. The Canadian Conservative Party vanished almost overnight, as did the Italian Christian Democrats, Socialists, and Communists. Mitterrand's Socialists were routed, as were the parties and movements of Africa's historic leaders, from Kaunda to Nyerere. In South America, the *caudillos* are gone, replaced with men and women calling for privatization, decentralization, entrepreneurship, and less control from the ministries and chancelleries. So strong is the popular desire for freedom that even those who once spoke the language of Lenin now recite Jefferson and Milton Friedman. Nelson Mandela emerged from his island prison still speaking warmly of Fidel and Qaddafi; today he privatizes and on occasion even calls for lower taxes. And everywhere there are new voices, new leaders, new newspapers and magazines, new television stations, and new forms of radio. An actor governed America, and a playwright leads the Czech Republic. A businessman replaced the Italian gerontocracy, and a trade union leader was president of Poland. Even the entrenched leadership in Japan is cracking, while a Japanese-Peruvian governs in Lima. Third, fourth, and fifth parties have appeared and disappeared, the vessels into which public disgust with the old order has been poured.

Just as the peoples of the Soviet Empire wanted greater freedom and brought down the tyrannical Communist system, so the peoples of the West today demand greater control over their own lives. Clinton placed himself against the revolutionary tide by reasserting the arrogance of the state. In one of the tragic paradoxes of this revolutionary era, two consecutive presidents of the United States, having lived through a global revolution inspired by American ideals, failed to seize their historic moment. It remains to be seen if Americans can recapture their faith in their revolutionary values and rally to the side of struggling democrats worldwide.

5

❖

THE STRUGGLE FOR UNDERSTANDING

The future of the Democratic Revolution is now in doubt. The advance of democracy is stalled, in grave danger of being rolled back. This is not a "clash of civilizations." The popularity of outspoken antidemocrats is not limited to nations under the sway of Islamic fundamentalism; they also hold court (and attract substantial electoral support) in Moscow, Minsk, and Bucharest. Without clarity of vision in the West and the will to pursue our historic mission, our antidemocratic enemies will gradually claw their way to positions of power and eventually use their strength against us. Even if today we cannot foresee the precise identities of the forces that will mobilize in that assault, we can be certain it will occur: tyrants cannot feel secure until we have fallen.

Roadblocks to the Democratic Revolution

Although the reluctance to proclaim victory and to continue to lead and inspire the Democratic Revolution is undoubtedly part of an understandable letdown after half a century of intense effort, more than mere fatigue lies behind it. Our leaders are not likely to soon forget the terrible stresses and, on occasion, devastating political shocks to which we were subjected. Men like Bush and Clinton remember the Vietnam years and, despite their very different attitudes toward the war, do not wish to repeat the anguish and turmoil of the Nixon and Johnson presidencies during their own tenure. Add to this dangerous brew the historical tendency of the American people to shun international engagement, and we get a potent toxin. Some elemental forces are also at work to the same end: the citizens of all modern, free societies are driven to challenge the legitimacy of their governments, even at moments of triumph. As François Furet has noted in his work on the Communist idea in the twentieth century, bourgeois hatred of bourgeois society is as old as the bourgeoisie and is an intrinsic part of modern democracy:

> The bourgeois . . . proclaims the universal, but carries doubt about the truth that he proclaims: a part of him yields to his adversaries, because they speak in the name of his own principles.[1]

The values of the Democratic Revolution, though universal, are never fully realized, for the messianic demands of freedom and equality conflict. Freedom creates both opportunity and inequality, and democratic capitalism will always produce new winners and losers. At every moment, therefore, the winners can be denounced as violating the ideal of equality, and the system itself will be branded as hypocritical. Our own history provides many examples of efforts to enforce political and economic equality, which in turn conflict with the freedom of others. Hence, even at our greatest moments we realize there is much to be done. As Furet has shown, the recognition of the conflict between freedom and equality produced a fissure through which the Communist idea penetrated modern democracy, presenting itself as the utopian fulfillment of the democratic dream.

Many, above all Western intellectuals, embraced this false messiah, and many such people denied the evils of the Soviet Union or discounted them as unfortunate false steps along the road to paradise. While bemoaning the "failures" of the Soviet system, these intellectuals held the final goal worthy and condemned as heartless reactionaries those who devoted their lives to the struggle against communism. Left-wing intellectuals found it inconceivable that the imperfect democratic societies of the West—especially the inelegant and chaotic American democracy—could prevail over the egalitarian ideal at the heart of communism. Thus, the "progressive" intelligentsia has predictably greeted the Western victory with uncomfortable embarrassment. How could it be otherwise? They had done so much to denounce our behavior, and explain away the Soviets', that the defeat of the empire was—or should have been—their defeat as well.

Rare is the person willing to admit error, and very few left-wing intellectuals have had the courage and candor to confess their analytical sins. When the distinguished Marxist historian Eugene Genovese wrote such a confession in *Dissent* in the spring of 1995— in which he passionately insisted that he and his colleagues had long known about the evils of Soviet communism but had consciously refrained from condemning them—his fellow-Marxists roundly denounced him.[2] Yet Genovese was right, and the failure of the Left to come to terms with its systematic lies about communism is part of the broader unwillingness of the American intellectual elite to acknowledge what actually happened in the epic struggle between communism and the West.

While Genovese's condemnation focused on the treatment of Stalin, the Left's coverup of the true nature of Soviet communism started at the very beginning of the Bolshevik seizure of power. As Jean-François Revel has reminded us, in the fall of 1917 and early 1918 the Moscow correspondent of the French Socialist newspaper *l'Humanité* filed a series of extremely accurate articles about the new Communist state, including the plans for the institutionalization of the Terror.[3] This information, and additional material along the same lines, was brought to the attention of the prestigious League for the Rights of Man in Paris, which was composed of some of the leading lights of the French Left. Their response prefigured that of the Western Left for the rest of the century. First, they appealed to the newspaper to stop publishing such damaging stories. Then, they found excuses for the Terror: encirclement by enemies, sabotage by the capitalist states, and so forth. All of this occurred long before the creation of the KGB's vast disinformation network that would hoodwink so many people in the years to come. This behavior was self-censorship, not Soviet cunning. The truth was readily available from day one of the Soviet Empire. The progressive intellectuals did not want to acknowledge it, because the truth would damage the cause of socialism and shatter the utopian myth of Communist revolution.

A similar conspiracy of silence was at work in the case of Mao Tse-tung's China. The dreadful purges that accompanied the Cultural Revolution were well known to reporters on the scene, but by and large we did not learn about them from the popular press until a moderate "thaw" was launched by Deng Xiaoping. To have told the truth would have destroyed the image of Chinese communism (and, not coincidentally, led to the expulsion of any journalist who dared write the story). The self-censorship extended well into the American academic community; a Stanford graduate student, Stephen Mosher, was excoriated by his peers and denied a Ph.D. for writing a dissertation that documented the practice of Chinese infanticide, favoring male babies over females.

In the context of the cold war, the suppression of damaging information about the Communist bloc was tantamount to favoring it at the expense of the West, about which no such comforting self-censorship was exercised. Much of the Left—both Marxist and liberal—did not want us to win, both because of their political commitment and because of a strain of anti-Americanism common to intellectuals of both political Left and Right. Intellectuals by and large hate the messy, inelegant ways of democratic capitalism—particularly America, the symbol of capitalist success. From the earliest days of the Industrial Revolution, intellectuals of all political hues felt humiliated by having to compete in the market. Enraged at being evaluated by unlettered readers, unworthy reviewers, and unsophisticated book buyers, they preferred to sit at the right hand of the Prince and engage in refined discourse with others of high standing.

Capitalism subverted the power of intellectuals, even those in Europe, who to this day have retained a degree of status and influence on politics that has generally escaped their American counterparts. American intellectuals are doubly affronted: first, because, like the Europeans, they are subjected to the same requirement to compete in the marketplace; and second, because, unlike the Europeans, Americans by and large do not esteem intellectuals. Envious of their European counterparts, American intellectuals feel belittled by their comparatively low status and prestige. America is held to be unworthy of the role history has assigned to it, and unworthy of its intellectuals.

The intellectuals' contempt for democratic capitalism leads them to favor central planning over free markets, despite the many successes of capitalism and the historic failures of central planning. The considerable intellectual support for command economies is part and parcel of the conceit that most problems are best solved by putting the best (that is, the smartest) people in charge of solving them. Whether in the form of the Soviet *Gosplan,* or the Japanese MITI, or efforts to centralize political and economic power in Western countries, intellectuals invariably applaud "solutions" enforced from above, because these methods are congenial to their own belief that they and their ilk are uniquely qualified to make the crucial decisions. It sounds good, after all: put the smartest people in charge of solving the toughest problems. What could be better? It is very hard for them to acknowledge that the markets are generally smarter than they are.

The Vogue of Japan. The brief intellectual vogue of Japan amusingly demonstrates the intellectuals' faith in the superiority of central planning. Until recently, Japan was treated as proof positive that rational planning was infinitely superior to the chaos of markets. The enormous wealth acquired by Japanese banks, the incredible value of Japanese real estate (at one point, Tokyo real estate was more valuable than that in all the United States), and the high quality of Japanese products were taken as evidence of American failure and the virtues of long-term planning. In early 1989, Jack Anderson darkly warned:

> From Manhattan to Waikiki, they [the Japanese] have bought up prime real estate and started up new plants. Japan is building a subeconomy in America that is out producing the regular economy.
>
> This could lead eventually to the collapse of American manufacturing. It also gives Japan a dangerous measure of control over our economy. Ever so subtly, control is shifting from Washington to Tokyo.

Pundits from Left to Right echoed these ominous prophecies, from liberal economist Felix Rohatyn to conservative publisher Malcolm Forbes, from journalists like Susan and Martin Tolchin to erstwhile strategist Edward Luttwak.

The prophets of American decline and Japanese ascendency were wrong. Instead of taking over, the Japanese were taken for a ride. In short order, the Japanese turned out to be the biggest dupes to come along since the oil sheiks of the mid-1970s. Nothing could convince them that glamorous American investments might possibly go sour. If a project were not immediately profitable, then they would put even more money into it, awaiting the inevitable bonanza. The symbol of the Japanese madness was the most costly resort hotel in the world, the Grand Hyatt Wailea on Maui, built at a cost of $762,000 per room. The accommodations are marvelous, the swimming pools are a dream, the eight restaurants are impeccable. The only problem is that, as the manager confessed several years ago, at 75 percent occupancy, with clients paying full rates ($375 per night), the place lost tens of thousands of dollars per day. The last time I checked, a travel package from Los Angeles, including air fare, was available for less than $150 per night at the Grand Hyatt Wailea.

The Hawaiian islands are littered with failed Japanese dreams of grandeur. The man who built the Grand Hyatt Wailea, Takeshi Sekiguchi, built a Four Seasons resort right next door and by 1991 was admitting to annual losses of $5–10 million. Across the water in Honolulu, the Waikiki Hyatt Regency was seized by the Mitsui Trust and Banking Company, after its customer, Azabu Building Company, could no longer make its payments.

Overall, according to Jack Rodman, who tracks Pacific Rim real estate markets, Japanese bank loans for American real estate will have to be written down more than 30 percent; and at least 70 percent of all the Japanese deals in the United States will have to be restructured or recapitalized, or taken over by Japanese parent banks, which often avoid meeting the more stringent international reserve requirements. The reality is likely worse than Rodman's estimates; according to the *Los Angeles Times,* many of the Los Angeles properties owned by the Japanese (even before the earthquake of January 17, 1995) had dropped two-thirds in value in five years or less.

It was only poetic justice that Japanese real estate investors took an enormous bath when they attempted to fulfill the vision of "taking over." They paid a steep price for their folly, but those who had hailed their infallibility were not called to account. When the Japanese equity and real estate markets crashed and burned and Japanese corporations found themselves struggling to cover their losses, our intellectuals—who hitherto had warned of the imminent Japanese conquest of the entire economic universe—did not announce that they had made a mistake or acknowledge that the American system had proved superior to Japan's. Instead, still hellbent on finding fault with the United States, they warned darkly of the terrible consequences, not for the Japanese—who were facing a massive systemic crisis—but for the *American* economy. This catastrophe did not happen. As with our victory in the cold war, the continuing success of the American system outraged a significant number of intellectuals.

Intellectuals, the Political Class, and the Media. All enemies of democracy hate the United States. In an earlier period, right-wing intellectuals were supporters of fascist leaders and regimes, and some of them passed from apologies for fascism to praise of communism, denouncing America all the while. The intellectuals of the Right emphasized America's lack of culture, its inconsistent attention to its global mission, and its lack of spiritual grandeur. Those of the Left stress America's presumed rampant capitalism, incurable racism, and near-Fascist anticommunism. They have had extraordinary success, to the point where even Ronald Reagan was forced to subdue his outspoken anticommunism. The tenacity and one-sided efficacy of the Left's condemnation of American anticommunism are well demonstrated by American cinema, which has given us dozens of movies about the victims of McCarthyism but not a single major film about the victims of Stalin. To be sure, American themes are more attractive to Hollywood than foreign ones, but there is no shortage of movies about the Russian and French Revolutions so dear to the Left. And, save for now-ancient pro-English films like *The Scarlet Pimpernel*, they are invariably favorable to the revolutionaries.

Despite the American tradition of paying relatively little attention to intellectuals, over the course of the past twenty years the intelligentsia has acquired greater influence over the political class, thanks to an effective working alliance with the elite media. As I have argued elsewhere,[4] American journalists have effectively become part of the executive branch of the government. Their offices are in government agencies, they travel together with top officials, and their primary objective is to shape policy. A seamless web binds together government officials and journalists, primarily because the press has demonstrated an ability to destroy politicians.

Journalists, who overwhelmingly share the values and

worldview of the intellectual elite, have become the long arm of the intelligentsia in Washington. In this classic symbiotic relationship, journalists receive the warm embrace of the academy, thereby heightening their self-esteem, and the academic intellectuals exert political power through their brethren in the media. The potential effect is enormous. George Orwell pondered the matter during the war against fascism:

> What has kept England on its feet during the past year? In part, no doubt, some vague idea about a better future, but chiefly the atavistic emotion of patriotism, the ingrained feeling of the English-speaking peoples that they are superior to foreigners. For the last twenty years the main object of English left-wing intellectuals has been to break this feeling down, and if they had succeeded, we might be watching the S.S. patrolling the London streets at this moment.[5]

We might well say the same thing about the cold war, for if our own left-wing intellectuals had had their way, we would have abandoned the fight against communism before its fall, with fatal consequences for Western democracy. That tradition continues. In keeping with the tight connection between journalism and government, Bill Clinton's longtime friend, former senior editor at *Time* and subsequently handpicked deputy secretary of state, Strobe Talbott, put it this way in his celebration of Mikhail Gorbachev in *Time* magazine on New Year's Day, 1990:

> The Soviet system has gone into meltdown because of inadequacies and defects at its core, not because of anything the outside world has done or not done or threatened to do. Gorbachev . . . has been discouraged and radicalized by what he has heard from his own constituents . . . not by the exhortations, remonstrations or sanctions of foreigners. . . . It is a solipsistic delusion to think the West could bring about the seismic events now seizing the U.S.S.R. and its "fraternal" neighbors. If the Soviet Union had ever been as strong as the threatmongers believe, it would not be undergoing its current upheavals.

The message is clear enough and could be repeated with dozens of examples: the fall of the empire was not our triumph but its failure. The entire worldview of the patriotic anti-Communists was utterly misguided, resting on an exaggerated notion of the danger posed by the Soviet Union. In Talbott's view, the cold war was not driven by the West's rational fear of Soviet expansionism but by a paranoid fear of a country that never posed a serious threat. Indeed, we are so unworthy that if the Soviet Union had been up to snuff, it "would not be undergoing its current upheavals." It is difficult not to hear a tone of regret in Talbott's words, as if to say that it would have been better if the Soviets had been worthy of their role. Then the intelligentsia would not have to cope with the annoying victory of democratic capitalism.

The media's whitewash of the Soviet Union has continued apace after the fall of the empire. In the fall of 1994, the *New York Times* ran a front-page story detailing the CIA's covert assistance to the Japanese Liberal Party during the 1950s. It was a classic of the genre, complete with embarrassed sound bites from the guilty politicians and apologetic remarks from the agency. The story was all based on declassified U.S. documents, nobody was denying it, and, while it was not today's news, it certainly warranted space.

The story came to the attention of Vladimir Bukovsky, the Soviet dissident, who lives in Cambridge, England. Bukovsky had recently returned from Moscow with a substantial quantity of KGB and Politburo documents, some of them providing evidence of an extended period of Soviet covert support for the Japanese Socialist Party, from the 1950s well into the 1970s.

Since the Socialist Party had only just entered the Japanese government for the first time since the war, and since such support was a violation of Japanese law, Bukovsky thought his information might find space in the *New York Times,* especially given its interest in the covert funding of Japanese politics. So he called Norman Podhoretz, editor of *Commentary,* who called Abe Rosenthal, former editor of the *Times,* who, after verifying the substance of the story, called (in his words) "the appropriate people" at the *Times.* And there the story died. The *Times* cared about an old story involving American covert support for a Japanese party but was not interested in a much more recent story about Soviet covert support for another Japanese party. It is hard to escape the conclusion that the *Times* editors were using political standards to evaluate the "newsworthiness" of the two stories, as in three others concerning the true history of the Soviet Union.

Soviet Intrigue in Greece. The first comes from Greece, where a tough *New York Times* writer named Paul Anastasi stumbled across one of the greatest of all the cold war stories, pursued it with dogged persistence and courage for many years, and—in keeping with the axiom "no good deed will go unpunished"—was rewarded for his efforts with a jail sentence. In 1978, one Yannis Yannikos, a veteran Communist Party member who had often been in the Soviet Union for months at a time since the 1974 fall of the colonels, showed up in Athens in search of a partner for a joint venture with the Soviets.

The plan was to launch a publishing house for Soviet books and magazines, with the financing coming from commercial joint ventures with Soviet corporations. Yannikos had been involved in the marketing of Soviet books in Greece in the past but was told by his Soviet interlocutors that this project could not be run entirely by a known Communist. He was urged to look for an appropriately non-Communist business partner. Yannikos came up with George Bobolas, a well-established businessman who worked mostly in import-export (and who bragged to the Soviets that he could help them with technology transfer, an area of particular interest to the KGB). Bobolas, who had fallen on tough times, was delighted to accept the Soviet offer: 70 percent of the profits from the commercial ventures would go into publishing, and the remaining 30 percent would be divvied up between the two Greek partners. Yannikos and Bobolas created the Academos publishing house, which promptly turned out one of Leonid Brezhnev's greatest hits and several volumes of the *Great Soviet Encyclopedia*. The returns were good enough for his Soviet friends to encourage Bobolas to embark on a new project: a daily newspaper called *Ethnos,* which he launched in the autumn of 1981, just a few weeks before the Socialist Party of Andreas Papandreou came to power.

Ethnos became the most popular newspaper in the country, a tribute to the degeneration of objective standards in Greek political and journalistic discourse. To call *Ethnos* pro-Soviet would be a considerable understatement. *Ethnos's* support for all things Soviet was so total that it often seemed to be a caricature, a sort of Platonic ideal of a Communist front publication. This newspaper did not blush at headlines like "The Soviet Woman Is Not a Feminist—She Has No Reason to Struggle Since All Her Problems Are Solved" or "The CIA Trains Mosquitoes to Poison—The Secrets of the USA's Biological War." *Ethnos* called the Soviet Union "the first peace bloc in history," claiming that the Berlin Wall was built to stop a planned NATO attack against East Germany first and eventually the Soviet Union itself:

> This wall would have been unnecessary if those who govern on the West bank of the River Elbe, as well as their Cold War allies across the Atlantic, did not and do not have as their permanent goal to devour the Socialist German state, and from there to continue to occupy "living space" in neighboring Czechoslovakia, Poland or even the USSR.

When *Ethnos* does not like the news, it simply spikes it (the pope's triumphal trip to Poland in 1983 was not even mentioned, except for one very short blurb from the Polish government spokesman). And it made certain there would be very little in the way of unpleasant reportage by hiring Communist Party or pro-Soviet editors and columnists. Its American commentator, Carl Marzani, who was a leading member of the U.S. Communist Party during World War II, later went to jail for three years when it was discovered that he had lied about his Communist connections while working in an intelligence unit in the State Department. Former KGB General Oleg Kalugin branded Marzani a paid KGB agent whose publishing house was kept afloat by Soviet money. The British correspondent was Stanley Harrison, who had been an editor at the official publication of the British Communist Party until 1981.

Nonetheless, *Ethnos* was a fabulous success, establishing new records for circulation and wielding enormous political influence on behalf of the Soviets. Bobolas, however, apparently on instructions from the Soviets, had cut the faithful Yannikos out of the deal. Yannikos was not pleased; he believed he was entitled to a share of the abundant profits from *Ethnos*. When Bobolas refused to ante up, Yannikos sued him and told the whole story to Anastasi.

Yannikos identified the three key movers behind the creation of Academos and *Ethnos:* Boris Pankin (director of the Soviet copyright office at the time and later deputy foreign minister under

Gorbachev), Vassili Sitnikov (deputy director of same and simultaneously deputy director of the KGB's Disinformation Department, specializing in propaganda operations against NATO), and Yevgeny Chistiakov (press attaché in the Soviet Embassy in Athens, a KGB operative subsequently expelled from Greece after being caught in flagrante trying to steal classified naval documents). Yannikos later told the *Wall Street Journal* that he had not realized he was dealing with the KGB at the time—a bit hard to accept from a man who had spent so much time in the Soviet Union.

Anastasi's exposé of the affair, *Take the Nation in Your Hands* (a minor pun, since *Ethnos* means *nation* in Greek), quickly became a runaway bestseller. *Ethnos* sued, receiving full support from the government: Anastasi's lawyer, who also served as legal adviser to the minister of youth, withdrew from Anastasi's defense on instructions from the minister just ten hours before the trial began. The Soviets brought pressure to bear as well; Sitnikov himself came to Athens to beg Yannikos to drop the suit, stressing how important *Ethnos* was to the cause. When Yannikos refused, Bobolas offered him $650,000 in exchange for his silence. Yannikos took the money and announced he was too sick to testify on Anastasi's behalf. Thus deprived of his key witness—the main source of the information in the book—Anastasi faced an impossible task. Although he had copies of some of the original documents provided by Yannikos (showing the genesis of Academos) and even though Yannikos' son testified as a defense witness (confirming, for example, Sitnikov's conversation with Yannikos *père*), he no longer had the kind of firsthand evidence that the court would obviously require. Anastasi was convicted and sentenced to two years' imprisonment. The sentence was reduced to one year on appeal, then commuted to a fine, which was ultimately thrown out by the Supreme Court on a technicality.

Ethnos's hysterical reaction showed that Anastasi had really hurt the organization, because Anastasi wrote for two of the English-speaking world's most prestigious newspapers, the *New York Times* and the *Telegraph* (London). Moreover, Yannikos had, for the first time, provided both documentary and firsthand evidence of the inner workings of the operation. *Ethnos* sued two European magazines that had picked up Anastasi's allegations: *L'Express* in Paris and the *Economist* in London. Both ended inconclusively, with both sides claiming vindication. And so the matter rested, until Bukovsky, looking through his cache of documents, discovered that he had several pertaining to the Bobolas affair. The documents antedate the creation of *Ethnos* by more than a year. The key document is a top-secret KGB report to the Central Committee of the Soviet Communist Party, entitled "On Cooperation with Greek Publisher G. Bobolas." It stresses the considerable value of Bobolas's activities, which it describes as part of the "active measures" campaign run by the KGB. *Active measures* is a term of art, referring to a disinformation campaign.

In that context, Academos is described as "the publishing base of ideological influence in Greece and among other Greek communities in other countries." It goes on to observe that Bobolas needed money to cover the operation and therefore recommends that the Ministry of Foreign Trade and the State Committee on Economic Relations should "render preference to G. Bobolas in deciding commercial questions under otherwise equal conditions." And the KGB also asked that Bobolas be given VIP treatment on his next trip to Moscow.

Five days later (April 10, 1980) two top Communist Party officials, Leonid Zamyatin and Vadim Zagladin, wrote the Central Committee along the same lines, describing Academos as a successful Soviet penetration in Greece. Other supporting documents repeated the same KGB position, and on that very day, a mere five days after receiving the original KGB recommendation, the Central Committee approved it. The document in question contains all the key signatures, from the top party ideologist Suslov and future dictators Chernenko and Gorbachev. In other words, support for Bobolas came from the very top of the Soviet pyramid, based on the recommendation of the KGB, which described Bobolas as an integral part of the disinformation campaign in Greece.

Bukovsky sent the documents to Anastasi, who tried to get Greek newspapers to pay attention to them. Unfortunately, the intimidation campaign waged by *Ethnos* and its friends in Papandreou's government had worked. Nobody was willing to become involved, until the secret documents were translated into English and described in great detail in two long articles in the *Swiss Press Review and News Report,* a highly regarded newsletter that was started in Geneva in 1959 to provide an independent source of information and commentary on international affairs. Once out in Switzerland, the information was quickly picked up by the conservative press in Greece. This time there was no legal action from *Ethnos* and no thuggish backup from the government. But the *New York Times* never ran the story.

At the time of the Anastasi trials in Greece, the *New York Times* gave complete coverage to its readers, cautiously defended Anastasi editorially, and sent strong supporting letters on behalf of Anastasi to the court. In response, *Ethnos's* lawyers demanded that the government investigate those foreigners who dared to write fairly—denounced by Bobolas's lawyer (previously Papandreou's minister of justice) as "a rabble of witnesses, British, German, Dutch, one Jew from racist South Africa, one American woman and former Greeks, who appeared in Greece as provocative, aggressive, impertinent advocates of the insultor and slanderer." The "American woman" was the *New York Times*'s own Marvine Howe.

The *Ethnos* story had everything a serious American newspaper should want: a fully documented look behind the scenes of international intrigue, a scandalous tale of governmental meddling with press freedom, an investigative journalist persecuted for telling the truth, and a dangerous collaboration between government and business to manipulate the media. If the American government had behaved in such a fashion, our editorial pages would be full of demands for special prosecutors, resignations, and impeachments. But the Soviet Union—even after death—was exempt from righteous indignation.

The KGB in the American Media. The Greek story intersected with a recent book about a highly regarded Western journalist working pen-in-inkwell with the KGB in Washington.[6] Written by Yuri B. Shvets, a former KGB officer stationed in Washington, it tells of the recruitment of a former member of Carter's White House staff and his wife, a journalist for several prestigious newspapers and magazines. It is obvious from the book, and from some heated correspondence between lawyers, that the woman is Claudia Wright, a regular *Ethnos* contributor and American correspondent for the *New Statesman* and *Témoignage Chrétien*. Her husband, John Helmer, worked at the International Center for Development Policy after Carter's defeat. The portraits of the two are quite unflattering: Wright is an unattractive middle-aged woman who "turned out to be a rabid antisemite as well as an enemy of

American conservatives. Her credo seemed to follow a simple formula: whatever is bad for the U.S. and Israel must be good." And Helmer "seemed to know and detest everybody and everything in this country." Helmer and Wright anticipate most of the KGB officer's moves, understand his operational problems, and act accordingly even without being asked.

The one exception to their willingness to do the KGB's bidding came when the KGB tried to get them to "bite" on a forged letter (sent anonymously through the mail) from the Heritage Foundation to Assistant Defense Secretary Richard Perle. Helmer would not touch it. "One scandal is enough for us," he said and a moment later added, "Experience tells us not to use anonymous letters anymore." The references were to an article that Wright had written in the *New Statesman* in 1982, based on a forged letter ostensibly from an official at the South African Mission to the United Nations to U.S. Ambassador Jeane Kirkpatrick, thanking her for all her "help," giving her regards from the chief of the hated military intelligence service, and alluding to a gift accompanying the letter. The forgery was sloppily done, and the State Department was able to expose it as disinformation, to Wright's great discomfiture. So Wright and Helmer were not going to fall for that sort of nonsense again. But Wright was delighted to take the KGB's line on arms control matters, on events in the Soviet Union, and on various other key issues.

Helmer's name will not ring many bells in the intellectual community, but Claudia Wright was rather high in such circles. If Shvets is telling the truth, Helmer wrote most of Wright's material for many years, as her Alzheimer's disease—which has left her non compos mentis in Australia (Helmer has long since jumped to Moscow)—intensified. Wright's name was certainly an influential one: the *New Statesman* has indubitably lost some of its luster since the days when the peerless Paul Johnson edited it, but it is still a prestigious publication and is widely read, particularly in academic circles. And Wright's poisonous disinformation appeared in some of America's most important publications: the *Washington Post*, the *New York Times*, the *Christian Science Monitor,* and even the flagship magazine of the Council on Foreign Relations, *Foreign Affairs.* Her writing appeared in numerous Arab publications around the world, as well as in the KGB's favorite newspaper, *Ethnos.* She was an ideal agent for the KGB because she did not need any convincing: she was already theirs, heart and soul. Her hero was Muammar Qaddafi, she dreamed of the destruction of Israel and the fall of America, and the only Soviets she did not like were those who were soft on Ronald Reagan.

This story raises two interesting points: the first is the conventional wisdom about Westerners who became KGB agents. According to this view, in the latter years of the cold war, nobody in the West was recruited on the basis of ideological conviction but on a sheer economic basis. Once upon a time a group of true-believing homosexual English Communists could easily be persuaded to commit espionage for the Soviets, but nowadays—or so the story goes—traitors do it for the money. If Shvets's account is true, however, Wright and Helmer fulfilled the Soviets' wishes for a long time, out of conviction; the money came later.

There is very little doubt that Shvets told the truth about KGB money being paid to Helmer, because before publication of Shvets's book, there was a lively exchange of letters and E-mail between lawyers representing Helmer and Simon and Schuster. When Helmer's attorney demanded to know what the book was going to say, the publisher's counsel responded with a list of questions for Helmer, including one about "receiving money from Tass or the KGB." Helmer's lawyer produced an amazing response: "As you will readily appreciate, there is a huge gap here. One claim is consistent with honorable conduct. The other charges one of the most serious crimes a citizen can commit." There was no denial from Helmer's side, and, despite repeated threats, there was no lawsuit when the book appeared, either. And it is probably just as well. Helmer could probably not be charged with anything approaching "one of the most serious crimes a citizen can commit," because, on Shvets's account, the information Helmer provided was not classified. In that case, he could not be charged with espionage—and mouthing or writing the Soviet line in public, although odious, is not a crime.

The real issue is not crime, but truth. Once Shvets's book appeared, all those who published Claudia Wright owed their readers the literary equivalent of a manufacturer's recall of a defective product. Her role as an agent of Soviet policy should have been fully exposed, and her editors should have expressed outrage and embarrassment at having been duped into believing that her thoughts and "facts" were as good as those of honest seekers of the truth. And in so doing, they should have demanded to know how many others had worked for the KGB, so that we could have discounted their writings as well. None of this occurred, and after a few book reviews, the Claudia Wright story quietly died out.

Anthrax in Sverdlovsk. The third example of the media's refusal to deal truthfully with the truth about the Soviet Union regards the mysterious accident in Sverdlovsk in April 1979, in which several hundred people died from anthrax. From the beginning, American intelligence experts were convinced that the epidemic was the result of an accident at a Soviet biological weapons facility. The Soviets vigorously denied it, insisting that the outbreak had been caused by some contaminated pork, not by any illicit preparations for biological warfare. It was an explosive issue, and it became even more so the following June, when a Soviet émigré by the name of Popovsky testified before a subcommittee of the House Intelligence Committee. Popovsky, the author of Soviet biology and medical texts, said that he had information about an explosion at Compound 19, a secret military facility in Sverdlovsk for the production of biological agents, at the time of the mysterious epidemic.

While most government scientists and intelligence analysts were convinced that Popovsky's information was good, there was one notable dissenter: Matthew Meselson, Harvard professor of microbiology, a consultant to the CIA on this very matter. Meselson later made a name for himself as the leading skeptic of the "yellow rain" theory. According to this theory, the Soviets were using poison gas against their enemies in Afghanistan, Laos, and Cambodia in the early 1980s. Meselson was also skeptical of the theory that the Soviets had facilities for biological weapons. His response was along familiar lines: first, I do not believe they did it; second, even if they did it, it would not necessarily violate the Biological and Toxic Weapons Convention (development of vaccines and antidotes was permitted, and so, perforce, was the production of small quantities of the agents themselves, in order to develop antidotes); and anyway I have an entirely open mind on the subject.

Meselson produced several learned theories to explain what had happened and to show that the explanation offered by the U.S. government was erroneous. The Soviets said that infection went on for quite a while, which suggested that the infectious agent was not a cloud of spores, since the cloud would have spread its poisons quickly. Meselson showed, from Soviet literature on the subject, that there had been many previous outbreaks of anthrax: thirty-five of them in Sverdlovsk between 1956 and 1968. So what was so surprising about yet another episode? This same theme was picked up by two Soviet scientists in the late spring of 1980 who wrote in a Soviet scientific journal that there had been 159 outbreaks of anthrax among livestock in the area between 1936 and 1979.

Nicholas Wade, writing in *Science*, supported that view:

> What is so inherently implausible about [the Soviet] explanation . . . ? The nature of the Sverdlovsk incident is still unresolved because the Soviets are still sulking. For that, the Administration is in part to blame. In effect, it has invited the Russians to sit down and discuss the issue with but one condition, that their explanation won't be on the agenda. . . . Without doubt, something strange and unprecedented happened. . . . It could constitute a violation—extraordinarily foolish and self-defeating— of the 1975 convention. But, with perhaps almost as much likelihood . . . it could have been caused by tainted meat, just as the Russians say.

Meselson appealed to the Soviet authorities to permit him to conduct investigations on the spot, and after four years, it appeared the trip would take place in the summer of 1983. At the last minute, however, hard on the heels of the KAL aircraft shootdown by the Soviets, the trip was canceled by the Soviet side. But three years later it was back on again, and in the summer of 1986, Meselson met in Moscow with the Soviet doctors who had examined the evidence back in 1979. They told him that the weather had been very bad around Sverdlovsk the previous summer, causing a reduction of fodder for farm animals; and local farmers had used various feed supplements that, in the past, had caused anthrax. Meselson looked at—and accepted at face value—hospital records that showed there had been a steady stream of victims, not a sudden surge of the sort to be expected from an accident. Meselson bought that explanation, and two years later organized an American tour for the doctors: Cambridge, Baltimore, and Washington, D.C. Meselson funded the event with money from a grant he had obtained from the MacArthur Foundation. Throughout, Meselson stressed the reasonableness and plausibility of the Soviet explanation, reserving an escape hatch for himself by stating that one could not be entirely certain until the military facilities in Sverdlovsk had been inspected.

Meanwhile, additional Soviet "sources" surfaced in the international press. Some were in predictably pro-Soviet magazines like the British *New Scientist,* but the stories ran almost everywhere. The *Financial Times*'s man in Moscow, David Satter, took a trip through the region in the spring of 1980, meeting various people whose anecdotal evidence supported the Soviet story. Finally, as pointed out by Thomas Whiteside in an overlong account of this and related stories in the *New Yorker* in February 1991, as late as 1989 Boris Yeltsin denied any military component to the Sverdlovsk incident, pronouncing the whole thing "natural." By that time, Meselson had become a hero of the anti-Reagan people because of his widely accepted claim that the Soviets had not used chemical or biological weapons in South Asia and that the "yellow rain" was really bee feces. In February 1990, Meselson was presented with the Freedom and Responsibility Award from the American Association for the Advancement of Science.

In the event, Meselson had been spreading disinformation. One of the first to suspect what had happened was David Satter, the *Financial Times* correspondent who had found sources to support the Soviet story on a trip through the region in 1980. "I now believe," he wrote in 1991, "that the people I quoted were KGB plants." He went on to add that, while he had found evidence that refuted the official version, it had inadvertently been edited out of his story. Satter was alarmed that articles like his own had contributed to the American decision in 1991 to drop the demand for "spot on-site inspections" of Soviet chemical weapons facilities as a condition for agreement to a treaty banning the weapons.

Satter reported the mounting evidence that the Soviets had falsified the "data" given to the West, had removed all records from the local hospitals, and had even had the topsoil removed, and the area asphalted, by workers wearing protective clothing. "Under the circumstances," Satter wrote, "it would be foolish for the U.S. to sign a chemical weapons ban. Such an agreement must be real, not imaginary. What Soviet disinformation efforts show is that we will not get real disarmament without strict verification and an insistence that . . . before they sign a new global ban, the Soviets explain why they violated the one that exists."

Far more detailed investigations appeared in the *Wall Street Journal,* penned by Peter Gumbel, and in the Soviet press itself. As early as the summer of 1990, just six months after the award to Meselson, the former organ of Communist disinformation, *Literaturnaya Gazeta,* presented firsthand accounts. One person, for example, is quoted as stating, "I am today firmly convinced that in the spring of 1979, a deadly cloud arose over our military center and the wind carried it." Horrible stories circulated at the time, about burying the dead in lead caskets and about research into genetic engineering; the Moscow publication quoted a local doctor who treated the victims of the incident: "What we had was waste from a bacteriological weapon."

Then in 1992, Yeltsin himself announced that he had been misled at the time but now knew that the incident had been caused by an accident at a chemical weapons facility. This admission galvanized Meselson into action. That summer he went back to Russia, and this time came up with evidence that, indeed, the cause of the anthrax outbreak had been airborne and not contained within rotten food. The *Harvard Crimson* reported the results the following year in the words of those who believe that only that which occurs in Cambridge, Massachusetts, can be taken seriously:

> Until today, officials in the former Soviet Union could claim that a 1979 anthrax epidemic . . . was caused by tainted meat . . . .But according to Cabot Professor . . . Meselson . . . the outbreak may have been caused instead by airborne spores. And if a military base near the site of the epidemic was the source, then the Soviets may be guilty of violating the Biological Weapons Convention of 1972.

No matter that the same information had been announced by the Russian president! There was no mention of the fact that the Cabot Professor had been pumping the Soviet line for more than a decade. Indeed, the *Harvard Gazette* of March 19, 1993, actually claimed that Meselson never had it wrong:

> Meselson, in 1986, finally received an invitation to go to Moscow and talk with doctors who had treated the victims. What they said about the cause of the epidemic

did not convince him, so Meselson invited the Soviet experts to come to the United States to talk with their American counterparts.

Moreover, Meselson still would not buy the line that the Russians were cheating on the treaty: "We can't assume violations," he points out. "The Soviets might have been working on a human vaccine against anthrax, something not prohibited by the treaty."

The public confession did not come until November 1994, when a group of American and Russian scientists published an article in *Science,* concluding that, just as the CIA had said from the beginning, the epidemic had been caused by escaping toxins from Military Compound 19 at Sverdlovsk. But the other shoe did not drop: no apologies for past error, no warning about the consequences of the discovery for arms control agreements, no agonizing reappraisal of the myth of moral equivalence.

And what about America's newspaper of record in all this? The *New York Times* had editorially embraced Meselson as one of the truly great scientific figures of the century, putting him on the same footing as Andrei Sakharov for his fight against chemical weapons. But the announcement in *Science* required some kind of reaction, so the *Times* called on one of Meselson's earliest aco-lytes, Nicholas Wade—now on the staff of the *Times*—and he re-sponded with an extraordinary puff piece in the *Sunday Magazine* of December 18, 1995. After a hymn to Meselson's work in chal-lenging the government's "yellow rain" hypothesis, Wade turned to Sverdlovsk, where, he noted, "The truth was not so clear cut" and Meselson "not so right." Indeed! No mention was made of the Meselson-sponsored tour by the Soviet disinformation team, and the whole thing ended on a high note:

> Meselson's new study puts a heavy burden on the Rus-sians to make clear what was really happening in Sverdlovsk and elsewhere. Moscow officials might as well yield those secrets now or they will face an indefi-nite siege. For from the lies of governments Matthew Meselson is determined to extract what he knows as a scientist to be true, that the pursuit of biological weap-ons is an extreme folly.

Instead of drawing the obvious conclusion—here is someone who has proved that he can be fooled by the Big Lie—the *New*

York Times took the opposite tack: the Russians better watch it! Anyone looking dispassionately at the record of the past sixteen years would have to conclude that Meselson, for the most part, had accepted the Soviet line. Most of his activities on Sverdlovsk (as on yellow rain) had consisted in attacking the United States and defending the Soviet Union. Meselson's considerable scientific and political prestige had gone to support the notion that one could trust the Soviets' statements on their biological weapons programs. U.S. government claims were far more suspect. When it turned out that he was wrong, the *New York Times* asked the same reporter who wrote puff pieces about Meselson's past errors to write the official coverup.

While there are some great reporters at the *New York Times*, it is hard to escape the conclusion that some of its editors do not want them to report all the news. This debate is not just academic; if the liberals, as exemplified by the *New York Times,* succeed in falsifying the historical record, the American public may well conclude that it was quite unnecessary for us to make great sacrifices on behalf of freedom during the cold war. It is a short step from that falsification of the past to an unwillingness to challenge the next enemy of freedom until he attacks us directly. It may prove fatal to leave the initiative in enemy hands. [7]

Failed Efforts of the Left

The efforts by the intellectuals of the Left to prevent our victory against communism failed, thanks to the good judgment of the American people. Gorbachev's frantic efforts to reform communism likewise failed, thanks to the good judgment of the peoples of the empire. Socialism has not ever been very popular with the American public, and there has never been a Marxist mass movement in the United States. Marxism failed in America in part because universal male suffrage was achieved before the Industrial Revolution (political identities were therefore established before class), and in part because of the success of capitalism. Very few Americans could be tempted to overthrow a system that they viewed as bringing greater wealth and satisfaction to constantly greater numbers of people. Furthermore, as Carl Degler has observed, there were patriotic reasons for the failure of Socialist ideology in the United States:

Some years ago an obscure socialist, Leon Samson, un-
dertook to account for the failure of socialism to win
the allegiance of the American working class.... Americanism, Samson observes, is not so much a tradition as
it is a doctrine; it is "what socialism is to a socialist."

Socialism has been unable to make headway with
Americans, Samson goes on, because "every concept in
socialism has its substitutive counterconcept in Americanism." As Marxism holds out the prospect of a class-
less society, so does Americanism.... Even the sense of
mission, of being in step with the processes of history,
which unquestionably was one of the appeals of socialism, was also a part of the American Dream. Have not
all Americans cherished their country as a model for the
world? Was not this the "last, best hope of earth"? Was
not God on the side of America, as history, according to
Marx, was on the side of socialism and the proletariat?[8]

The American people rejected the leftist utopia that so entranced many intellectuals. On the eve of the 1984 elections, James
Reston of the *New York Times* wrote a revealing column in which
he mused that never before had so many in the media worked so
hard for the defeat of any presidential candidate as he and his
colleagues had strived to beat Ronald Reagan, but all had been for
naught. Reagan won in a landslide, in no small part because what
Orwell called the "atavistic emotion of patriotism" remained the
dominant one in the United States. Patriotic passion also played a
role in the election of Bill Clinton, who during the campaign of
1992 portrayed himself as tougher than George Bush. The revolt
against Clinton came only when he revealed himself to be just as
weak-kneed as his predecessor.

Understanding the Cold War

The instincts of the American people, like those of the peoples of
the new democracies, lie with the Democratic Revolution. But they
are baffled and frustrated by the ineffective policies of their leaders. Of all the failures of Western leadership, none is so grave as
the failure to explain in detail precisely what happened during the
twentieth century, especially the years of the cold war. If, as the
intellectual Left is so desperately arguing, the defeat of tyranny

was not due to the moral and political superiority of democratic capitalism, then the West, and especially the United States, has no right to claim global leadership. This dispute is therefore not merely academic: at issue is the legitimacy of America's role as the lone superpower in the post–cold war world.

The most reliable sources for understanding this matter are those who struggled against tyranny: the Solzhenitsyns, the Bukovskys, the Havels, the Walesas, the Mandelas, and the Juan Carloses. All of them were inspired, to varying degrees, and with different levels of knowledge and understanding, by the American model. Their struggles for freedom were not merely acts of defiant resistance: they knew there was something better. Sometimes their knowledge came from short-wave radio, sometimes through underground publications, and sometimes through a network of trusted friends. Sometimes their expectations of America were wildly unrealistic, but all knew that, without America, they were doomed, and that, willy-nilly, the United States had lent strength to them and their cause. Even in cases like Bukovsky's, where years of living in the United States left him profoundly embittered by our repeated failures to take appropriate action against the Soviet Empire that had subjected him to nearly two decades of torture and imprisonment,[9] America was denounced for failure to live up to its own highest ideals, for its betrayal of the revolution, not because it was fundamentally on the wrong side of history or because it had insufficient moral and political standing to lead the fight for freedom.

As in the debates over the nature of Italian fascism, the struggle to define the nature of the cold war has as much to do with control over the future as with pure understanding of the past. If the critics of anticommunism succeed in institutionalizing their view that the United States and its allies were wrong to resist and ultimately roll back Soviet communism, American political culture and American public opinion are most unlikely to support a vigorous international policy in support of the new democracies and those yet unborn. If, however, the moral conflict at the heart of the cold war is widely recognized and acknowledged and the victory of the West over the Soviet Empire is embraced and celebrated, that will provide the moral and political basis for the further advance of the Democratic Revolution.

Some evidence suggests that the intellectual tide is turning. Just as the leftist vogue in Europe was discredited by writers like

Alexander Solzhenitsyn, Raymond Aron, Jean-François Revel, and Renzo De Felice, so the false stereotypes of the American Left are now eroding, and the purveyors of the myths are losing their charisma. It is now possible to challenge even the most cherished myth of the Left: that anticommunism was intrinsically evil and that all anti-Communists were McCarthyites.

That concept was definitively debunked in *The Secret World of American Communism,* published in mid-1995 by the Yale University Press. *The Secret World,* a collaborative effort between two American scholars and a Russian archivist-historian, is based on the archives of the Central Committee of the Soviet Communist Party. Its story is the worst nightmare of the anti–anti-Communists: the American Communist Party actively recruited espionage agents for the Kremlin, who sabotaged American national security and then lied about it when caught, manipulating the "useful idiots" in the liberal press, universities, and government to attack their accusers as totalitarians, while they were actually guilty of that very crime.

Predictably, the elite media downplayed the significance of the book. The *Washington Post* carried a quiet, purely descriptive story well inside the first section, with no editorial comment, and the *New York Times* did the same. In the past, one would have expected vigorous attacks on such a publication, but there was no such challenge to *The Secret World* (perhaps because the evidence came from the Soviets themselves). Few issues are of greater significance to our national consciousness, for the Soviet documents show that many leading members of a crucial generation in contemporary American history were liars and traitors who damaged the country and falsified its history for over a half-century. The Left can no longer dismiss the gravity of its actions by pointing to the outrageous behavior of the McCarthyites, for anticommunism is vindicated by the evidence in the Soviet archives.

Much of the truth we need to know about the twentieth century still lies in the archives of the former empire, a truth desperately needed on both sides of the old Yalta line. I have already underlined the importance of the Soviet archives for the citizens of the empire, but they are equally important for us. We must understand what we were up against and who were our real friends and enemies. Vladimir Bukovsky was enraged to discover that the Russian government had decided *not* to release the list of foreign journalists who collaborated with the KGB, and his anger was justified. It is necessary for the West to know the difference between honest journalism and either gullibility or active service on behalf of the other side. The real history of Soviet communism and the cold war is the context within which we must evaluate our contemporary leaders and our future foreign policies. We must understand the nature of our enemies, so that we can judge whether our sacrifices were worthwhile, which of our policies were well judged, and which were misguided. Above all, we must understand the nature of the confrontation with the Soviet Empire: an ideological clash between two messianic visions.

The Silence of the West

The silence of the West on these matters, of a piece with its unconscionable silence on the sealing of the Soviet archives, constitutes a terrible blow to the future of the Democratic Revolution and an enduring embarrassment to all those in a position to insist that the truth be told. Those networks, newspapers, and magazines who fought so hard for "freedom of information" in the United States and in other democratic countries did not feel obliged to denounce Yeltsin's decision to seal the archives. Yet they are the first to blast any CIA director who tries to keep a limited number of American secrets. Threatened by the truths about the Soviet system—truths they denied for so long—the traditional elites act as our censors, all the while posing as the most zealous defenders of "the people's right to know." It is a desperate holding action but probably one destined to fail. Not only is the ideology of the Left out of steam, but its ability to control the flow of information to the public has been seriously undermined.

The three major television networks, which once dominated the flow of information to American households, have seen their popularity steadily dwindle and are reducing their staffs. The major newspapers and weekly news magazines have similarly lost market share and have cut back on personnel. At the same time, the voices of the democratic counterculture have become more powerful. In the first two years of the Clinton administration, both the *American Spectator* and the *National Review* enjoyed an explosion in circulation (the *Spectator* went from about 30,000 subscribers to more than a quarter-million in two years). A new conservative magazine, the *Weekly Standard,* exceeded all its original expectations in circulation and advertising after its launch in the autumn of 1995.

These clear indications of the growing strength of believers in the superiority of democratic capitalism, along with the enormous popularity of Rush Limbaugh's conservative talk radio program and others that piggybacked onto his success, showed that the American public was profoundly dissatisfied with the worldview of the elite media. It was as if the American people had known that they were not getting the truth but did not know where to find it. Once they were given real choices, they turned away from the tainted sources. One of the most notable developments in this story is the surprising popularity of C-SPAN, which broadcasts live, uninterrupted coverage of events. The appeal of C-SPAN is obvious: it eliminates the filter of the broadcasters, journalists, and editors between the news and the citizen. Observers collect their own information, firsthand, and draw their own conclusions. Some of the excitement about the Internet has the same basis, for it gives individuals the ability to scan the world's databases and to judge for themselves what is important and what is not. This global shift is unlikely to die out in the near future. Despite the desperate efforts of the traditional elites to falsify history and convince the electorate that problems are better solved by the state than by the people, the bankruptcy of the traditional elites is so manifest, and the desire for untainted sources of information so widespread, that the fall of the old media will continue, as will the rise of the new.

The Cultural Shift

Two basic and important differences lie between the way in which the cultural shift occurred in Europe and in the United States. In Europe, a handful of intellectuals and political leaders produced spectacular changes in the popular culture, while in the United States no single individual, or small group, drove the change. Instead, dozens of think tanks, scores of individual writers, broadcasters, actors, and producers and grass-roots political, cultural, and religious organizations have transformed the political debate. Retaining their august status, European intellectuals still exercise considerable control over the political debate, which is one reason why Western Europe today is by and large absent from the global dialogue about the future of democratic capitalism. The conviction that the "smartest" people should make society's decisions is stifling to the kind of rapid-fire, trial-and-error, market-driven world that is coming into being. The West Europeans are having a hard time weaning themselves from the good old days of *dirigisme*. The most vigorous experiments with democratic capitalism are more easily found in Asia and the Americas than in the Old World, and West Europeans may have to take their inspiration from South Koreans, Chileans, and Americans to move forward in the near future. The political leadership in such countries has decided to trust the people, privatize as many government functions as possible, and get out of the way: no West European government would take a similar course. The European leader who is closest to the vision of the new order is Prime Minister Vaclav Klaus of the Czech Republic.

The second difference has to do with religion. Men and women of deep religious faith were central in many of the successes of the Democratic Revolution. The pope's global role has been discussed earlier, and reference has been made to organizations like Opus Dei, the Catholic group that supported liberal reforms in Franco's Spain. There were others, of which key Solidarity leaders like Lech Walesa are perhaps the best known. But with the exception of the pope and Alexander Solzhenitsyn, it is hard to find religion at the forefront of the political debate in Western Europe. The opposite is true in the United States. As Robert W. Fogel, the Nobel laureate from the University of Chicago, has pointed out, 74 percent of "evangelical or other believers in enthusiastic religion" voted for Republicans in the 1994 elections:

> If those who embrace enthusiastic religion turn out in the same proportion in 1996, and if they continue to favor the Republicans over the Democrats by the same margin, there will have been an inter-party shift of about 7.5 million voters. That shift by itself is enough to create a 14 point spread in the upcoming presidential election in favor of the Republicans.[10]

Fogel views this shift as part of a fourth Great Awakening, a mass religious revival of a sort that has already dramatically shaped American politics and society three times in the past, most recently in the Social Gospel that emerged from the Third Great Awakening at the turn of the twentieth century and laid the moral and philosophical basis for the New Deal. The passions at work in the current religious revival are remarkably similar to those that have driven the Democratic Revolution: "It is fueled by a revulsion with the corruption of contemporary society. . . . The leaders of the revival are attempting to win their hearers to piety and to an ethic which extols individual responsibility, hard work, a simple life, and dedication to the family."[11] Inasmuch as the state is viewed as profoundly corrupt, the Great Awakening is intensely antistatist.

Fogel is not alone in believing that evangelical Christianity is a very important political force in America in the mid-1990s. Irving Kristol takes Fogel's theory one step further, proclaiming that the Republican Party soon will effectively be led by Christian activists. Walter Dean Burnham, who has long stressed the centrality of religion in American political dynamics, tells us that the 1994 election "was but the latest stage in a politics of upheaval that became visible around 1990. A vast and accelerating public discontent with government and political establishments then cascaded through the system."[12]

Although there is no comparable phenomenon in Western Europe, religion has played a major role in East and Central European politics. Pope John Paul II's role in the flood tide of the Democratic Revolution was enormous. Even though the influence of the Roman Catholic Church has ebbed in the intervening years, much of the political and moral discourse is framed in religious terms. President Havel of the Czech Republic, for example, sounded very much like an American evangelical when he said, at Liberty Hall, Philadelphia, on the Fourth of July, 1994:

> Only someone who submits to the authority of the universal order and of creation, who values the right to be a part of it and a participant in it, can genuinely value himself and his neighbors, and thus honor their rights as well. . . .
>
> The Declaration of Independence, adopted two hundred and eighteen years ago in this building, states that the Creator gave man the right to liberty. It seems man can realize that liberty only if he does not forget the One who endowed him with it.

Advancing the Democratic Dream

The surge of religiously inspired people is a further sign of the disintegration of the worldview (along with the legitimacy) of the established elites.[13] According to a global consensus, collectivism has failed, and the immediate future of civilized nations will take the form of democratic capitalism, with due allowance for cultural variation. This is the victory of the Democratic Revolution. But it is a fragile victory, and it has been blocked and even reversed in many countries, because we have not yet achieved full understanding of our own history and because our leaders seem not to know where to take us. The first is a grave problem, which may in the end prove fatal to some of the new democracies. It will undoubtedly weaken all of us, even in the face of considerable progress. The second is actually a blessing in disguise.

For a brief moment, from the mid-1970s to the late 1980s, a generation of spectacular leaders inspired and catalyzed the Democratic Revolution: Pope John Paul II, Ronald Reagan, Margaret Thatcher, Lech Walesa, Vaclav Havel, Nelson Mandela, F. W. De Klerk, King Juan Carlos, Mario Soares, and Adolfo Suarez. Although the destruction of tyranny from Iberia to Latin America, from Central Europe to southern Africa could not have been accomplished without great leaders, the essence of the Democratic Revolution is that, once the tyrants have been destroyed, we no longer need central guidance to fulfill our democratic destiny. It is no accident that the triumph of the revolution has produced a sharp fall in the quality of leadership. Two centuries ago Alexis de Tocqueville realized that democracy in America led to mediocre political leaders, an insight abundantly confirmed. We will not be led by great men and women except in rare moments, and that is the way it should be. The question before us now is whether the citizens of the democracies, new and old, can further advance the democratic dream and assume responsibility for their own lives.

6

❖

THE FUTURE OF THE REVOLUTION

The political universe is still in the grips of powerful revolutionary forces, as demonstrated by the worldwide crisis of the old democratic elites. In early 1996, there was hardly a civilized country in which the mighty were not subjected to the humiliation of a judicial inquiry or parliamentary investigation. In India, so many politicians were being dragged to trial that a new party was born, the Party of the Guilty. Elsewhere, for the most part, the accused fought on.

The Clintons had a special prosecutor, scores of investigative journalists (the first books on Whitewater were just hitting the bookstores), and zealous senatorial and congressional inquisitioners. Former Italian prime minister Silvio Berlusconi faced trial in Milan. Former Spanish prime minister Felipe Gonzalez was compelled to schedule the early elections that ended his long tenure because of parliamentary, journalistic, and judicial investigations into financial and antiterrorist wrongdoing. French politicians and businessmen across the political spectrum have been destroyed by judges, and in Belgium two former foreign ministers and a former defense minister fell to investigations into political payoffs from military contracts (one, Willy Claes, lost the post of NATO secretary general). Polish Prime Minister Jozef Oleksy was forced to resign during investigations into his previous KGB connections, and Colombian President Samper called for an investigation into his own campaign's financing. Former officials of South Africa's military were standing trial, and there were mounting calls in the South African Parliament for similar investigations of Nelson Mandela's African National Congress. The world's most scandal-ridden democracy, Japan, lurched from one shocker to the next as politicians and governments came and went with startling frequency.

Former top officials and current business leaders were standing trial in South Korea, and a wave of suicides accompanied parliamentary investigations into corruption in Taiwan. Former president Salinas of Mexico was under investigation, as were the former presidents of Peru and Venezuela and the former Italian prime ministers Giulio Andreotti and Bettino Craxi, the latter long since having taken refuge in Tunisia. Scandinavian political leaders' half-life diminished by the month. In America, the Democratic congressional whip and two Democratic speakers of the House of Representatives had fallen from power, the former chairman of the powerful House Ways and Means Committee faced trial, and the current Republican speaker was under investigation. It was a global purge, the latest phase in the global Democratic Revolution.

The Sources of Corruption

The cold war provided opportunity, motive, and "cover" for much political and economic corruption. Most democratic countries were unwilling to put their political leaders under the microscope, fearing they would destabilize and weaken the state and open the doors to Communist tyranny. Thus, the political and business elites, which acquired a near-monopoly of political and economic power, held it far longer than they would have under normal circumstances. This overlong monopoly led to the vast system of corruption documented in the purge trials and investigations. It is surely no accident that the two hitherto most "stable" political and economic classes in the West—the Italian and the Japanese—now vie for the title of most corrupt.

The corruption of the West was not limited to the conservative anti-Communist parties. The democratic challengers from the Left had been brought in and had eagerly gobbled up a share of the wealth. The German Social Democrats and the French, Italian, and Portuguese Socialists raced to get their share of the booty when they entered government, often surpassing their political opponents in amassing ill-gotten gains (the Italian purge, to date the most devastating, began with investigations into the Socialist financial empire in Milan). By the end of the cold war, they were part of the system.

Italy offers the clearest example of this process. From the end of World War II until the end of the cold war, Italian politics were dominated by the presence of the largest Communist Party in the Western world, the PCI (Partito Comunista Italiano). Between 1948 and 1991, the Communist share of the national vote was roughly one-third, making it the second largest party in Italy. At times, it appeared that the PCI might force its way into the government: first in 1948 and then again in the mid-1970s. On each occasion the elections constituted a national referendum on the legitimacy of the PCI as a governing party, and each time the Italian electorate voted no.

The rejection of the PCI left the country by default in the hands of the Christian Democrats (DC), which in truth was not so much a party as an amalgam of fiefdoms, factions, and special interest groups. No matter: the DC was the linchpin of every postwar government until the spring of 1993; and since power corrupts even its briefest holders, the Christian Democrats—whose tenure is unequaled in the history of European political parties— became profoundly corrupt. The corruption of the DC and its various coalition partners was not merely political; much of Italian business was owned, wholly or in part, by the state, and much of private Italian business came from dealing with the state. It was impossible to say where "government" ended and "business" began.

By the mid-1980s, huge commissions—sometimes reaching as much as 30 percent—were built into government contracts (especially public works) and then divided among the companies, who shared their take with the political parties. *All* major parties participated; the Communists were cut in (adding to the funding provided them by the Soviet Union and to the commissions they earned on projects carried out by Italian companies in the Communist bloc and pro-Communist third world countries) along with the others. According to published testimony, for example, the Communists were given the entire payoff from the Milan subway system, and they transferred half to the Socialists and a quarter to the Christian Democrats. This evidence was confirmed in court in the spring of 1996, when Bettino Craxi, the former Socialist leader, was sentenced to eight years in jail for the payoffs and the chief Communist financial officer, Gianni Cervetti, was sentenced to two and a half years.

It was an efficient and democratic corruption, for the payoffs were divvied up roughly in accordance with the relative strengths of the parties. Although everyone knew the system existed, no one made a serious effort to challenge it, for two very good reasons. First, despite its cost (those commissions came out of the pockets of Italian taxpayers, after all), it was extraordinarily successful: this corrupt system brought Italy from the ruins of the war to become the world's fifth industrial power. Second, the Communist alternative seemed far worse politically and was no less corrupt. So it was that "Tangentopoli" (payoff city) prospered on the banks of the Tiber, the Po, and the Arno, until it was destroyed by an unexpected moral earthquake in the early 1990s.

Craxi and the Socialists. The epicenter of the quake was Milan, which had become a stronghold of the Socialist Party (PSI, the Partito Socialista Italiano) and its leader, Bettino Craxi. This tough political animal knew about political earthquakes, having himself unleashed one in the late 1970s when he captured control of the PSI from a group of lackluster holdovers from the days of the alliance with the Communists. Craxi transformed the PSI into an outspokenly anti-Communist, pro-NATO party. It was a great success for the party, the country, and the Atlantic Alliance: the PSI delivered the crucial votes to approve the installation of U.S. cruise and Pershing missiles in Europe in the late 1970s. Above all, Craxi and his party effectively blocked the Communists' drive to national power.

By the early 1980s—when his term as prime minister was the longest of any postwar government—he had become the John F. Kennedy of Italian politics, and in Milan, as in Rome, the most glamorous women, the elite of Italian cinema, the new pinup stars of Italian business, and the heroes of Italian soccer joined the party. The most effervescent symbol of the Craxi years was his friend, Foreign Minister Gianni De Michelis, who, with his long hair and vast midsection, his witty repartee and constantly changing cast of gorgeous female companions, charmed and scandalized Western capitals.

Had they been more attentive to the risks of power, the Socialists might have become a durable force for generations to come, but they were in a great hurry to cash in on their success. The stories of Socialist enrichment bring to mind the legendary day in Kinshasa when the Zairian dictator Mobuto Sese Seko gathered his scandal-ridden ministers around him and gravely intoned, "Gentlemen, this is not the way one is supposed to steal." So far as is known, no such sermon was delivered to the leaders of the Italian Socialists.

The Socialists, of course, were doing only what all the others had long done, but there was a widespread conviction that the PSI's greed produced a Hegelian leap of quantity to quality and that Socialist corruption was far worse than the previous varieties. In February 1992, the separated wife of a Milanese businessman who had been making payoffs to local Socialists brought charges against him. The investigating magistrates followed the money trail, which led them into a vast network of commissions, bribes, and payoffs, largely in the hands of Socialist Party officials and their business associates. In short order, politicians and businessmen were slammed unceremoniously into prison, the investigation was expanded to cover the whole country, and the scandal spread to include leaders of all parties and their business allies. The bell that tolled for Craxi tolled also for the DC, the PCI, and most all the smaller parties. It was the Great Purge, Italian style.

The instrument of the Great Purge was the judiciary, which not only hears cases but also investigates allegations to determine whether they warrant a trial. This might seem similar to an American grand jury, but the two institutions are polar opposites. The grand jury simply decides if an indictment is justified, whereas the investigative magistrate can arrest people (and have them held—on extremely vague charges—for up to two years) and order police to search domiciles, seize documents, and even tap telephones. The grand jury is supposed to protect citizens against arbitrary state power, whereas the investigative magistrate *is* the state, with all its menacing powers at his full disposal.

In practice, the Italian magistrates threw many of their key targets into prison and let it be understood that the hapless souls would be released only if they pointed the way to juicier targets. With such "tools" at their disposal, it was not surprising that the magistrates obtained thousands of "confessions" nor that many of these confessions failed to stand up in court.

The Italian Revolution. Despite the relatively small number of criminal convictions, the political effects were devastating. The Socialist Party was shattered; in the June 1993 municipal elections, the PSI virtually disappeared north of Rome, drawing slightly more than 1½ percent of the vote in Milan, its previous stronghold. The other traditional parties, including the Communists (now split into a Stalinist rump and a reformed Party of the Democratic Left) were similarly afflicted. Parliament quickly hammered out a new electoral law, retaining some elements of the old proportional method while providing for winner-take-all voting districts for three-quarters of the deputies and senators.

The new parliamentary elections in the spring of 1994 featured the emergence of a new political figure: Silvio Berlusconi, a real estate tycoon, media magnate, sports impresario, and former intimate of the unfortunate Craxi. Less than three months before the elections, Berlusconi announced the creation of a new conservative political movement (Forza Italia, which is what sports fans yell at the national team when it takes the field) and forged an electoral alliance with the Northern League (an antiestablishment and sometimes separatist party from Milan, which had become the biggest party in the north) and the National Alliance (a newly crafted, more democratic version of the old neofascist party). Berlusconi's slogans were right out of the Reagan and Thatcher playbook: lower taxes and smaller government. This unlikely troika won the elections, achieving a fragile majority in the Chamber and falling barely short of one in the Senate. As prime minister, Berlusconi put together a group of largely new faces (only two of his ministers had held such rank before), to match the change in the legislature (only one-third of the parliamentarians had held such positions in the past).

Although he was an unlikely revolutionary, Berlusconi was in a position to transform the relationship between Italians and the state radically, and his campaign promises suggested he understood the possibilities. His rhetoric anticipated the Contract with America that was so effective in the American congressional elections later in the year. Had he been able to reduce taxes and privatize large chunks of the vast state-owned businesses, the nature of Italian society would have been fundamentally changed. The power of the old political elite would have been definitively broken, for the state, deprived of its control over everything from insurance companies to gas stations, would no longer have been able to provide the funding for the political parties. Businesses would have had to respond to the demands of shareholders rather than taking their instructions from politicians and bureaucrats, and normal citizens would have had more of their income to spend as they wished.

After a few months in office, Berlusconi's defining moment arrived. His justice minister issued an executive order, limiting the use of preventive detention by the judges. From the standpoint of civil liberties, it was a desperately needed measure and conformed to the standards laid down by the European Union, which Italy was formally obliged to meet. But the decision kicked off a political firestorm, as the judges took to national television and Berlusconi's opponents, supported by a frenzied campaign in the popular press, accused him of trying to rein in the judiciary to save his own companies and members of his family from the consequences of judicial investigations. Berlusconi backed down, thereby sealing his fate. Within eight months of taking office, he was forced to resign.

Two years later, a left-wing coalition, led by the former Communist Party and including many recycled Christian Democrats from the old days, captured Parliament in new elections. For the first time since the onset of the cold war, the Left—albeit, as in Central Europe, a Left speaking the language of democratic capitalism—would govern Italy.

Difficulties of the New Democracies

The failure of the Berlusconi experiment was of a piece with the defeat of many of the new democratic forces elsewhere in Europe. After a brief moment of glory, most of the democratic anti-Communists, after halfhearted efforts to transform their centralized, state-owned economies into largely privatized, market-driven systems, were voted out of office and replaced with former Communists. The Poland over which Lech Walesa once presided now has a president and parliamentary majority of the old guard, as do Hungary and Bulgaria. The old Communist elite never left power in Romania. Yeltsin has sounded less and less a democrat, and former Communists in Russia are no longer ashamed to praise the good old days when Stalin ruled and life was orderly. The brave

Lithuanians, perhaps the most outspoken anti-Communists in the final days of the empire, were the first to vote the old Communists back into power. Of the more than 300 million citizens of the Soviet bloc, all but slightly more than 20 million lived under governments with former Communists in control of either the legislature or the executive, or both, by mid-1994. The trend continued well into 1996, leading many to predict that the former Communists would win the Russian presidential elections in June.

One could go through the countries one by one and find errors, even very grave ones, committed by the new democrats, in an attempt to explain their rejection by the voters and the surprising comeback by people who were left for dead on the political pyres of the early 1990s. But the dimensions of the phenomenon are so impressive that more general explanations are required:

• First was the lack of preparation of the new democrats for the task of governing. Men like Walesa in Poland, Dimitrov in Bulgaria, and Landsbergis in Lithuania were brilliant as leaders of anti-Communist movements but were not well equipped to deal with the far different and more complicated questions of guiding the transition to democratic capitalism: from privatization, restitution, and restructuring of the public sector to managing the difficult personal and political conflicts that erupted within their own ranks. It is not surprising that the democratic talent pool was relatively shallow. After World War II, the victorious Allies were very pessimistic about the possibility of finding sufficient qualified democrats to govern Italy, Germany, and Japan. Indeed, George Kennan—the director of policy planning in the State Department at war's end and author of the celebrated essay that popularized the "containment" doctrine—recommended keeping many Nazis and Fascists in office, because the few democrats that did exist had no government skills. This, only twenty years after Mussolini's march on Rome and a mere dozen after the National Socialist seizure of power in Germany! The Communists were in power in the Soviet Union for nearly eighty years and in the Central and East European satellites for nearly half a century. To be sure, Kennan was wrong; there were plenty of talented democrats in Italy and Germany. The problem was a real one, though, and it was much harder to find democratic talent after the fall of communism than after the defeat of fascism.

Moreover, most of the democratic leaders were viscerally conservative. Having been deprived of religion, they sought it out and embraced it. As victims of intolerance and repression, they bent over backwards to give their opponents maximum opportunity to speak and organize. And, as victims of an evil "revolution," they shied away from the mobilization of the masses that had been the hallmark of the totalitarian regimes of the twentieth century. Believing their success to be irreversible, they learned the hard way that the course of history is not preordained and that every victory must be earned.

• Second, the new democrats underestimated the skill and tenacity of the former Communists. Like most of the rest of the world, they expected the old Communists simply to wither away, but this did not happen (save in Czechoslovakia). Instead, the members of the *nomenklatura* clung desperately to the levers of political and economic power and used their enormously superior political skills and experience to sabotage the democrats. In Bulgaria, for example, Dimitrov's parliamentary majority rested on a coalition with the Turkish Party, but the former Communists had infiltrated that group so successfully that they were able to thwart most of Dimitrov's efforts at radical reform and voted him out of office in a year. In Russia, Yeltsin had to cope with a Duma that was firmly under control of the former Communists. In Poland, the solid anti-Communist majority in the Sejm was quickly gutted by internal wrangling, catalyzed in part by Walesa's awkwardly heavy-handed methods. And some of the heroes of Solidarity, like Adam Michnik, unexpectedly demonstrated greater sympathy for the old leaders than for Walesa and the new democrats, thereby confirming Joseph Conrad's melancholy observation in *Under Western Eyes* that

> the scrupulous and the just, the noble, humane, and devoted natures; the unselfish and the intelligent may begin a movement—but it passes away from them. . . . Afterwards comes the turn of all the pretentious intellectual failures of the time.

• Third, the democrats were held accountable for the failures of the old regimes. With the exception of Czechoslovakia, every country in the old empire was bankrupt at the time of the fall of communism. The new governments had to struggle not only to meet the costs of converting to a free market but also to pay off communism's staggering debts. In the last years of communism, international lenders had poured a fortune in aid money into countries like Bulgaria and Romania (the Bulgarians owed $12 billion at the time of the fall of the Zhivkov regime), for which the new governments were held strictly accountable. Even today, it is hard to imagine the wreckage inherited by the democrats (in Bulgaria, for example, a square meter of linoleum cost more than a square meter of land throughout the Communist era).

• Fourth, the political damage inflicted by communism was greater than anyone had imagined. The prime minister of Bulgaria at the time, Phillip Dimitrov, put it so eloquently:

> Five decades of communist rule left our people not only with an incredibly corrupt and oppressive political system and a shattered economy, but also with a value system or [sense of] civic virtue that was seriously damaged. It is in this crucial aspect of civilized society that our people, and indeed all of Eastern Europe, were most seriously wounded.[1]

• Fifth, the Western countries often acted as if the greatest threats to the emerging democracies were not the iron grip of the old elites but the emergence of a new nationalism. In keeping with their old slogan, "no enemies on the left," most American and West European intellectuals were quick to support self-proclaimed Socialists and social democrats, while branding conservatives as dangerous nationalists and warning darkly of the emergence of new forms of fascism and nazism. This stance was more than an overreaction; it was exactly backward. There was no Fascist revival (there were just some hoodlums who wore Nazi or Fascist costumes, but not a political force), but there *was* a comeback of the old Communists.

The Communists Return to Power

Although the messianic mission of the world Communist movement had failed, the Communist cadres did not forget how to manipulate the levers of power. The competition with the inexperienced, well-meaning, and tolerant leaders of the new democratic parties was no contest. On the one hand, the Communists delayed and sabotaged the transition to democratic capitalism, while, on the other, they denounced the new democrats for incompetence and indifference to the pain inevitably caused by the transition. The Great Purge cleansed the political and business elites of the democratic countries but not those in the countries where purges were most desperately needed: in the states of the former Soviet Empire, above all, in Russia itself. Corruption in the West was child's play compared with corruption in the Communist dictatorships, and the prime forces of corruption in the Communist bloc rode out the democratic wave and then recaptured political power.

As Anne Applebaum has told us, "It is not the specter of the 1930s that haunts Central Europe, but . . . corrupt regimes led by former communist parties that rely on a semi-mafia business class composed mostly of former communists."[2]

The overthrow of the Ceausescu regime in Romania—hailed at the time as an integral part of the anti-Communist revolution— was the classic example of the triumph of the Communist bureaucrats. Indeed, according to Ion Mihai Pacepa, the former head of the Romanian intelligence service,[3] the "transition" in Romania had been planned years before by the Soviets and then carried out by the very people recruited by Moscow, much as the short-lived *glasnost* regimes in East Germany, Poland, and Hungary. General Nicolae Militaru, who proclaimed himself the head of the armed forces within hours of the Ceausescus' attempted escape, had met with a Soviet intelligence officer in 1978 to plan an anti-Ceausescu coup. Ion Ilitch Iliescu, the post-Ceausescu Romanian president who dropped his middle name after the overthrow, had been endorsed by the Kremlin as the most suitable leader of the Romanian Communist Party. Silviu Brucan, the "ideologist" of the National Salvation Front, "publicly acknowledged that [the coup] had Moscow's blessing, which he had brought back with him from a 1988 visit to the Soviet Union." The Salvation Front government was virtually indistinguishable from what had existed under Ceausescu: five cabinet members had been at the upper levels of Ceausescu's *nomenklatura,* and at least eight others had been key collaborators with the security services. No significant changes were made in the armed forces or at the upper levels of the public sector industries.

The Exception of the Czech Republic. The exception that proves this unhappy rule is the Czech Republic, where there has been no resurgence of the former Communists. In large part, credit goes to the excellent leadership with which the country has been blessed: Klaus and Havel combine the best of tough-minded structural reform with inspirational democratic conviction. The roles played by these two are strikingly similar to those played by Juan Carlos and Adolfo Suarez in Spain, with Havel serving as a kind of spiritual leader and Klaus managing the day-to-day affairs of the government. Of all the post-Communist transitions, the Czech is most like the Spanish model that inspired so many democratic revolutions around the world. Unlike most of the other new democrats, both Klaus and Havel understood that they not only had to guide the structural transition but had to explain the reasons for their decisions and win and sustain a national consensus. Klaus was constantly on television, debating his critics, and traveled widely outside Prague to take his case directly to the public. Klaus also embraced the felicitous idea of distributing vouchers to all citizens, enabling them to obtain shares in newly privatized companies. Since voucher holders had a wide range of choices for their investments, the program served as a stimulus for citizens to study the actual condition of Czech businesses and actively engaged them in the transition.

Other factors contributed to make the Czech story unique. Alone of the bloc countries, Czechoslovakia had no significant foreign debt at the moment of the fall of communism. Alone of the bloc countries (excepting Romania), the fall of the regime was sudden; there was no extended period of *glasnost,* during which the Communist Party could shed its totalitarian skin in favor of a more democratic one. The Czechs got lucky when the country split in two, since Slovakia had five times the unemployment of the Czech Republic, the bulk of the uneconomical heavy industry, and a far higher inflation rate. Unlike most of the other bloc countries, the Czech Republic had had pre–World War II experience as a modern nation, with a long history of advanced commercial codes, modern banking methods, and the other building blocks of civil society. This tradition lasted until the Nazi invasion. Thus, although Czech industry was retrograde by Western standards, it was the most advanced of the East European countries. Moreover, the country's proximity to Germany gave it a ready market for its low-cost products, and industrialists were eager to open factories there to take advantage of the low-cost (one-fifteenth that of Germany in the early 1990s) but well-educated Czech work force.

Finally, Czechoslovakia (and East Germany, which, because of its absorption by the Federal Republic, does not really count) was the only country to try to eliminate former Communists and collaborators from positions of power. The so-called lustration policy undoubtedly led to acts of injustice and, as Havel wryly observed, sent some little fish to prison but did little to punish the major offenders. By and large, however, it did give greater opportunity to those who never collaborated—in contrast to countries like Russia, Poland, and Hungary, where the state apparatus remained firmly in the hands of the former Communist *apparatchiks*—and it forced the Czechs to confront their own history. The country's success can be gauged by its recent renewal of Klaus's government for another five years, which must mean that the Czechs believe its overall effects are good for the country, and by the fact that the democrats in the Czech Republic are politically stronger than those in any other Central European country, not to mention Russia.

The Rout of the Russian Democrats. The extreme case of rollback of the new democrats at the hands of the old corrupt *nomenklatura* was Russia, which came very close to becoming the first major Mafia state in the world. It may not be possible to reconstruct precisely the details of this fascinating process, but by the mid-1990s a significant proportion of the Russian economy was run by organized crime. The mechanism itself is easy enough to understand. In the beginning, the ruble became the laundry soap of choice for international narcotics syndicates and other criminal organizations eager to obtain cash that could not be traced back to its Western source. Even though the double transaction (hard currency to rubles and then back) might entail commissions of 20 to 30 percent, the crime syndicates were willing to pay it. Soon, however, they learned an even better use of the Russian currency.

In 1990–1991, a combination of Mafia sharks, Soviet and Russian governmental officials, Western businessmen of dubious moral character, and KGB officers organized a variety of schemes to buy enormous quantities of rubles at cheap, black market rates and then purchase Russian raw materials with the discounted rubles to export the commodities, tax and duty-free, for multiple markups in hard currency. At one point in late 1990, the sums involved in formal negotiations with the Russian government added up to more than the entire amount of rubles in circulation! Most of the schemes collapsed, but many succeeded. As a result, the crash of the ruble accelerated, effectively bankrupting the Russian treasury. At the same time, the entire Soviet gold supply was spirited out of the country and sold for private gain, thereby depriving the government of desperately needed reserves to shore up the currency and adding further momentum to the crash. [4]

The corruption of post-Soviet Russia was carried out by a combination of the old *nomenklatura* (particularly the intelligence services), international organized crime, individual entrepreneurs from many countries, and members of the new government,[5] greatly aided by the failure of the Russian government to move quickly to create a market economy. Some of the documents unearthed by Vladimir Bukovsky and Claire Sterling suggest that the Soviet elites had an organized plan to export the wealth of the old empire to provide a base for themselves. Whether such a scheme was actually carried out, or whether the sacking of the natural resources of the Soviet Union was largely the result of latterday robber barons seizing a golden opportunity, the outcome was the largest one-time transfer of wealth in the history of the modern world.

Needless to say, very little of this wealth benefited the average Russian. The "new class" of Russian businessmen was overwhelmingly composed of the old Communists. Much of this catastrophe could have been avoided by a timely move to a market economy by the new government. If the ruble had been quickly made convertible on the open market—as the zloty was, for example, in Poland—it would have found a relatively stable level, and the Mafiosi and their Russian compadres would not have been able to count on the massive collapse of the currency, which created the enormous spread between the ruble's purchasing costs and the hard currency sales revenues. Instead, trapped as they were in their old attitudes, neither the Gorbachev nor the Yeltsin team was able to make any meaningful progress toward the transformation of the Soviet system, either to improve the ethics of the ruling class or to introduce a market economy.

The Russian case is extreme, as one would expect from the country subjected to the longest span of totalitarian terror. In most of the other bloc countries, the old Communists were able to sur-

vive only by ostensibly converting to the democratic faith and brag-
ging about their Western credentials. Polish Prime Minister
Wlodzimierz Cimoszewicz, for instance, has made much of his five
years at Columbia University, as Foreign Minister Dariusz Rosati
has of his Fulbright year at Princeton in the late 1980s. Thus,
while the old guard is back, they are back in new clothing and
carrying out policies they branded as anathema less than a decade
ago. Even though the democrats have suffered political setbacks,
their view of the world remains predominant, as can be seen on
the other side of the old Yalta line: Bill Clinton is running for
reelection as the man best able to fulfill a kinder and gentler version of the Republicans' revolutionary agenda, and the new "leftist" governing party of Italy speaks enthusiastically about increasing
the tempo of privatization.

Wishful Thinking. That so many are prepared to accept these con-
versions as genuine bespeaks a triumph of hope over experience
that is easier to understand in the former Communist countries
than in the West. After all, communism had violently distorted
modern history to justify the enslavement of its subjects. It was
too much to expect that the newly liberated millions of the old
empire could catch up with the truth in short order, especially as
the West lacked the self-confidence to educate them. As Michael
Radu has described it, the legacy of communism was

> an infantile ersatz culture of rejection . . . based on igno-
> rance, cynicism, and a vague longing to be part of the
> rich, but not necessarily the capitalist and democratic,
> West. Belief in the short-cut and the emergence of a true
> "me generation" of nihilists were the unintended results
> of communist education rather than the intended "new
> man." Neither did it produce the anti-communist demo-
> crats Western conservatives had hoped for. What it did
> produce was a huge crop of amoral, anti-ideological,
> and apolitical youths. It was a generation with no
> memory of the past, no interest in it, but also no stake in
> the present; a generation of aimless opposition. When
> old communism collapsed, this generation felt orphaned
> as much as it felt free.[6]

What else could it have been, and how else could it have felt?

Those tempted to condemn the new democrats for the failure to achieve a rapid, smooth transition to democracy had their perspective distorted by the success of democracy in Spain and Latin America, forgetting that recovery from the evils of relatively short-lived traditional authoritarianism is a lot easier than recovery from many decades of modern totalitarianism. The world was inspired by the examples of Spain and Portugal, but it was also misled. The success of the Democratic Revolution in the Latin world, followed by the unexpectedly peaceful collapse of communism, tempted us to believe that an irresistible process was at work and that people everywhere not only *wanted* freedom but understood how to achieve it.

Exodus, Old and New. The oldest case of transition from slavery to freedom—the liberation of the Jews from Egypt—abundantly demonstrates the profound difficulties in overcoming the slave mentality. After crossing the Sinai and reaching the border of the Promised Land, the Jews insisted that Moses send spies ahead to check on possible difficulties. God, though annoyed that anyone would doubt His promise to give the Jews a land flowing with milk and honey, approved the plan. Joshua then led twelve men, carried out the surveillance, and returned after forty days. They all reported that the land was indeed rich and beautiful, but ten of the spies, who warned that the inhabitants were bigger and stronger than the Jews, heavily armed, and superbly fortified, urged that the mission be abandoned.

They suggested that the Jews return to Egypt, which, while difficult, was at least not a threat to life. Joshua and Caleb disagreed, reminding the people of the many miracles that brought them out of Egypt and across the Red Sea and the vast desert. But the people turned on their leaders, demanded the removal of Moses and Aaron, and attacked them with stones. God was forced to intervene to save the four leaders and decided (albeit only after Moses talked Him out of His original plan to destroy the ungrateful Jews and start a new people with Moses and his family) that not a single one of those over twenty years of age would be permitted to enter Israel. They were sentenced to wander in the wilderness for forty years—one year for each day of the spy mission. The forty years would serve as a quarantine to liberate the people, once and for all, from their servile mentality—ready to collapse before the slightest difficulty just to get a loaf of bread—to look more carefully at the vast horizon of life, and to learn that one acquires and sustains liberty only when all together are agreed to defend this great common good.[7]

With such a precedent, it should not surprise us when many of the former slaves of the Soviet empire would lose faith in the future after several hard years along the path to democracy, vote to remove the men and women who led them after the escape from communism, and even contemplate a return to slavery. A free society cannot be sustained by citizens who cannot think freely, and the slave mentality cannot be overcome overnight.

The Spanish and Portuguese people were never totally cut off from Western culture. A sizable part of the population had participated in fairly open debate about the political future, particularly in the last years of the dictatorships. Morever, the democratic leaders who followed the collapse of the Franco and Salazar regimes had all received excellent educations, had devoted much time and energy to planning the transition to democracy, and were fully prepared for their mission.

Far more arduous, the post-Communist task required leadership of the highest order, recalling Henry George's description of Moses:

> To lead into freedom a people long crushed by tyranny; to discipline and order such a mighty host; to harden them into fighting men . . . to repress discontent and jealousy and mutiny require some towering character— a character blending in highest expression the qualities of politician, patriot, philosopher, and statesman.

Leaders with such rare qualities were unlikely to emerge in any, let alone all, the countries of the former Communist bloc. It is little short of miraculous that some did, from Klaus and Havel to Pope John Paul II. Lacking such leadership from within, the best hope was that it come from the West, primarily from the United States. Sadly, it was not to be, and most of the new democracies embarked on their own extended quarantine in the desert between slavery and freedom.

The Examples of Taiwan and South Korea

The Czech case is anomalous, and the Iberian and Latin American countries faced quite different challenges from those faced by the post-Communist countries. We still have no model for the successful transition from totalitarian dictatorship to democracy; the most successful examples are those from authoritarian tyrannies to democracies. And in this context, the cases of Taiwan and South Korea are quite instructive.[8] Although neither was ever a totalitarian system, both were governed for many years by harsh military dictatorships and lacked any firsthand experience with democracy. Yet by 1996, both had become democracies in spectacular and totally unexpected ways. Taiwan's elections in April 1996 were the first time a president of anything called "China" had ever been chosen by popular suffrage—a national experience stretching back some five thousand years. And South Korea had become one of the world's most outspoken advocates of democratic capitalism, had put its previous rulers on trial for their past sins, and was publicly challenging Singapore to a contest to see whether an open society or a tightly managed one was best suited for global competition.

Despite their geographic proximity, the two arrived at democracy in entirely different ways. The transition in Taiwan was carefully designed by the old autocrats and then carried out on schedule. In South Korea, democracy was won from below, concession after concession extracted from the rulers by broad-based street demonstrations, intellectual protest, and labor strikes. The Taiwanese transition began in 1985, when president Chiang Ching-kuo (the son of Chiang Kai-shek) announced that it would be unconstitutional for any member of his family to succeed him and inappropriate for the presidency to pass to a military officer.

The following year he empaneled a commission on political reform, thereby indicating his willingness to support such reforms. By October, Chiang announced that martial law would soon be lifted and new political parties would be created. Martial law indeed ended in July 1987. After a lull in the tempo of reform following Chiang's death in January 1988, movement resumed two years later when his handpicked successor, Lee Teng-hui, abolished the law that had indefinitely postponed national elections. Shortly thereafter the Council of Grand Justices ruled that all parliamentarians that had been elected on the mainland—the survivors of the Communist takeover and the hard core of the ruling elite—would have to resign by the end of the following year. Elections for a new parliament were held in December 1991, which gave Lee's party a resounding vote of confidence, while electing several representatives from the leading opposition party. Less than four and a half years later, President Lee was democratically elected, completing the transition.

The Transition in South Korea. In South Korea, democratization began in the spring of 1987, after the government refused to permit leading opposition figures to stand in the elections later in the year. Student protest had always been tolerated—as in many Latin American countries—but the demonstrations against the government's decision quickly spread throughout the population. The governing party's designated new leader, General Roh Tae Woo, astonished the country by announcing he would lead his party only if completely open elections were held and the new president were directly elected by the people (heretofore the parliament named him).

Roh managed to eke out a plurality victory in a three-way contest and then had to govern for most of his five-year term with a parliament in which his party lacked a majority. He played the game, negotiating policies and personnel decisions with the opposition, and his own successor was forced to compete for the party's votes in a wide-open, sometimes chaotic party congress. By 1996, the democratic transformation was so thorough that Roh himself was arrested for corruption and a national catharsis was underway as an investigation opened into the massacre of hundreds of civilian protesters by the army in the city of Kwangju in 1980.

Breaking with the Past. Despite the considerable differences between them, South Korea's and Taiwan's democratic achievements required a break with their antidemocratic past and the exclusion of many former tyrants from the countries' political life and governmental infrastructure. In Taiwan, the national leader ordered it, while in South Korea, it came about as a result of popular pressure from below. Whatever the method, the step was decisive. In both cases, about ten years were required to accomplish the transition. Those concerned about the slow pace of progress in the former Soviet Empire can take heart from the Korean and Taiwanese examples. The desert is long and the trek is difficult, even in countries in excellent economic circumstances, when there is no democratic culture.

The urgency and fragility of the revolutionary imperative—with its dual components of change in spirit and a real transformation of government and society—are wonderfully captured in an essay written in the fall of 1993:

> For the first time in our history, there is a broad consensus in favor of a predominant role for civil society and private enterprise . . . not only in the economic sphere, but in the institutional life of society as well.
>
> This is new. Our tradition, and it is a very old one, has been that all aspects of life must fall under the responsibility of the state. . . . It was thought to be the only guarantor of efficiency and justice, despite the opposite experience of the state being the source of inefficiency and corruption.[9]

These words could describe any of the old Communist societies of the former Soviet Empire, but they were written by the Latin American novelist, Mario Vargas Llosa, about the dramatic changes that had taken place in his part of the world. The process is the same, everywhere.

South Korea and Taiwan are often invoked in support of the thesis that democracy follows national enrichment, and certainly both countries were on impressive upward growth curves during the decade of political transformation. But it is well to remind ourselves that the claim of a causal relationship between wealth and democracy is not convincing, even in Asia. If wealth causes democracy, why has Singapore retained its oppressive political system? And, turning to another continent, those who believe that Western sanctions against the apartheid regime in South Africa hastened the arrival of the democratic era must agree that in this case misery, not enrichment, greatly assisted the Democratic Revolution in that land.

The magic formula for successful transition is as simple to state as it is difficult to find: great leadership, either from above or below. Just as the Soviet Empire fell when the leaders in the Kremlin had a collective failure of nerve, so fledgling democracies succeed when leaders decide that the people are worthy of trust and that genuine political legitimacy can derive only from the consent of the governed. The transition to democracy begins with an act of faith in the people's right to decide, continues by submitting to their verdict, and is fulfilled by reducing the power of the state, thereby expanding the freedom of all citizens.

Two hundred years ago, in the Age of the First Democratic Revolution, limiting state power meant restricting the arbitrary authority of the feudal institutions: church, monarchy, and aristocracy. Today it means waging war against the growing power of the preeminent modern institution: state bureaucracy.

Bureaucracy

While the threat of bureaucracy was evident nearly a hundred and fifty years ago to the French and Russian anarchists, the first systematic analysis was produced by a group of unorthodox political thinkers in Italy: Gaetano Mosca, Vilfredo Pareto, and Roberto Michels. The last, a German Jew who made Italy his adopted home, was a Socialist, but by 1911 his studies had led him to the horrifying conclusion that European Socialist parties—which Michels had hoped would bring democracy to the continent—had been taken over by professional oligarchies, thereby subverting the democratic goals of the movement.

Although they continued to preach the virtues of democracy and equality, the Socialist parties were neither democratic nor egalitarian. They had come under the rule of what Michels called the Iron Law of Oligarchy. He prophetically concluded that "the socialists might conquer, but not socialism, which would perish in the moment of its adherents' triumph." Mosca grimly observed that "all political regimes are of necessity ruled by . . . an organized minority controlling a disorganized majority." Thus, whatever the political goal of party or government, the show is run by the oligarchs, that is, the bureaucrats.

A brilliant, long-forgotten French historian by the name of Emmanuel Beau de Leaumenie reached similar conclusions. His voluminous series on the French bourgeoisie chronicled the amazing survival of the French bureaucracy from Napoleon to the era following World War I. By painstakingly tracking the family histories of hundreds of French civil servants, Beau de Leaumenie was able to prove that the actual management of French government had remained in the hands of a few hundred families through a period that encompassed the Revolution, the Napoleonic Era, the restoration of the monarchy, the bourgeois revolutions of the early nineteenth century, the Second Empire, the restoration of "bourgeois democracy" after the fall of Napoleon III, and the Great War. Kings were beheaded, emperors came and went, revolutions surged and subsided, but the bureaucrats remained untouched, their hands firmly on the levers of political power, their jobs—and thus their power—passing quietly from father to son. In our day, the most dramatic example of the Iron Law of Oligarchy is Russia and some of the other countries of the old empire, where, just as in France, the *nomenklatura* maintained its power in the face of a political revolution.

America was the last of the Western nations to fall into the clutches of the bureaucrats. By the 1950s, though, C. Wright Mills realized that power in Washington had been transferred from elected officials to the bureaucrats, who constituted a new "power elite":

> The executive bureaucracy becomes the arena within which and in terms of which all conflicts of power are resolved or denied resolution. Administration replaces electoral politics.

This lament has grown in intensity with the passage of the years, as the bureaucracy has expanded and enforced its Iron Law on us. Once Congress realized how powerful the executive bureaucracy had become, it created its own. Today, the federal bureaucracy alone (not counting the military bureaucracy, which is a horror story of its own) numbers more than 3 million persons. State and local bureaucracies account for an additional 15 million (and these numbers are undoubtedly low, because they include only salaried employees).

In his masterpiece, *Parkinson's Law,* C. Northcote Parkinson traced the relationship between the growth of bureaucracy and work actually performed. Parkinson first saw the light while studying statistics on the British Admiralty between 1914 and 1928, a period that saw a decrease of 68 percent in the number of ships, a drop of 31 percent in the number of officers and sailors, and yet an increase of 78 percent in Admiralty officials. Parkinson then turned his attention to the Colonial Office and found a similar pattern: it had grown from a mere 372 in 1935 (when there was a substantial empire) to 1,661 in 1954, when there was hardly an empire left. The inescapable conclusion was that bureaucracy always expands, independent of its tasks.

The enduring horror of bureaucracy, however, lies not in its numbers or even its cost, but rather in its effects. Bureaucracy is antithetical to enterprise and innovation and thus to freedom itself. As Ludwig von Mises observed, when a leader delegates tasks to his subordinates, the leader loses power, and his position is automatically threatened and limited by the subordinates. So, to limit the power of the subordinates, rules and regulations are issued, and this is the magical event: "Their [the subordinates'] main concern is to comply with the rules and regulations, no matter whether they are reasonable or contrary to what was intended. The first virtue of an administrator is to abide by the codes and decrees. *He becomes a bureaucrat.*"

The Iron Law applies, regardless of the views of the political leadership. It matters little whether the government is liberal or conservative, Republican or Democrat, Left or Right; the bureaucracy, like the sorcerer's apprentice, moves relentlessly and tirelessly forward.[10] That is why the call to slash the size of government is such an integral part of the Democratic Revolution.

America's Contract with the World

The Republicans' Contract with America, the set of promises on which Republican Party candidates ran in the congressional elections of 1994, was a declaration of war against the vast federal bureaucracy and its allies among the lawyering class. The landslide Republican victory showed how strongly that theme resonated with the American people. Few Republican leaders saw its international significance, however, as was demonstrated by the lack of any coherent Republican foreign policy in the following two years.

Yet the success or failure of the war to expand individual freedom in America is a matter of great consequence for the entire world, because the American example sets the course for much of mankind and because our mission is universal. Other countries can deal separately with foreign and domestic policies, but for us there can be no dividing line. We need better schools because without superior education Americans cannot fulfill a global mission. We need greater freedom so that the creative energies of the American people can continue to stimulate and enrich mankind. We need to repudiate the divisive radical separatists, from the feminist remnant to racial nationalists and the Nation of Islam, so that we can demonstrate with renewed vigor that citizenship, not ethnicity, faith, class, gender, or race, is the proper basis for civilization.

At the same time, we need to renew our assault against the enemies of democracy, and for this we require both domestic success and economic and military power. The world has not turned toward democracy merely because everyone has suddenly seen the light. The Democratic Revolution succeeded in part because of our military power and our ability and will to use it successfully. There were hot battles in the cold war, and, after Vietnam, we won most of them: we defeated the Soviet Empire and its surrogates in battle from Grenada and Angola to Afghanistan and Nicaragua. On other battlefields—most dramatically in the Middle East—our allies, fighting with our weapons, defeated Soviet allies fighting with theirs. When Israel demolished the Syrian air force over Lebanon in 1981, it was a triumph of American military might over Soviet military technology and advisers, just as it was when we crushed Saddam Hussein a decade later. Political power does not come exclusively from the barrels of guns, but if our enemies have bigger guns, we will be at a considerable political disadvantage. We want to be top dog.

It is symptomatic of the confusion of the established classes that, when policy planners in George Bush's Pentagon reiterated this self-evident principle of foreign policy in the spring of 1992, it was assailed as if it had come from *Mein Kampf*. America-bashers, long regretting our military might, considered it unclean. They wish to slash our military strength and expand the domestic bureaucracy (they call it "guns for butter"). These are false alternatives. If we are serious about supporting the Democratic Revolution, we must insist that the principles of the American Revolution be enforced at home and abroad. At home, we must fight to reclaim power from the state; abroad, we must be strong enough to support democratic revolutionaries fighting to reclaim freedom from the tyrants. If we are strong and show the nerve and wisdom to support the enemies of tyranny, then the democratic revolutionaries will take heart and will risk the challenge. If we are weak and indecisive, the tyrants will take heart and destroy their democratic opponents—and ultimately direct their evil impulses against us.

Redrawing the World's Map. We will have many opportunities to support democracy in this turbulent period. It was both inevitable and desirable that the world's political map should be redrawn, for much of the old order was artificially imposed on peoples who would never have voluntarily agreed to it. Stalin dealt with the "nationalities problem" in the Soviet Union by a combination of mass murder, repression, and forced migration. Some of the survivors wish to reclaim their ancient lands, and we should honor their desires. Most of the world's borders were established, either as the result of colonial bargains or as the result of war—the border being established between opposing armies at the moment of truce. Despite the formal boundaries, some groups feel themselves part of a different unit and wish to live together, either as a separate polity or as a highly autonomous part of a larger entity.

The established borders sometimes divide tribes and peoples or religious and ethnic groups that logically and historically belong together. The extreme case is Africa, where borders, imposed by Western colonial powers, divide tribes and peoples. If the Africans were free to choose their borders, they would undoubtedly do some drastic restructuring, and we should encourage them to do so. As two distinguished scholars have pointed out, the agreement of people to the physical domain of their state is logically and historically prior to the establishment of democracy:

> The very definition of a democracy involves agreement by the citizens of a territory, however specified, on the procedures to generate a government that can make legitimate claims on their obedience. Therefore, if a significant group of people does not accept claims on its obedience as legitimate, because the people do not want to be a part of this political unit . . . this presents a serious problem for democratic transition and even more serious problems for democratic consolidation.[11]

The disintegration of the old order—even on our side of the Yalta line—goes hand in hand with the defeat of communism, for our own political decisions have long been conditioned by the presence of a deadly enemy. From the rise of fascism until the fall of the Soviet Empire, elections in the free world were constrained by the fear of totalitarianism. We needed big government to protect us from mortal threats to our survival as a free people: first fascism, then communism. So we made a Faustian pact, accepting big government as the price of winning the war against evil. Having defeated the enemies who threatened the very existence of democracy, sovereign peoples will naturally reevaluate their governments. That is why even the boundaries of the Old World are being called into question. Basques and Catalans, Scots and Sardinians, Flemings and Walloons are demanding greater autonomy and sometimes even independence. The breakup of Yugoslavia was not a unique case. In the Italian parliamentary elections in April 1996, the biggest vote getter in the north was the Northern League, whose demands for greater autonomy from Rome and disgust at paying the bills of the Sicilians and Calabrians often verge on separatism.

It is not only traditional national units that face an uncertain future. Large multinational institutions such as NATO and the European Union were created to defend against the threat of war in a bipolar world. Their *raison d'être* having vanished, their advocates now insist that "economic necessity" requires their continued advance, but the economic models that inspired the theory of "necessity" are now in serious trouble. The remedies for the current economic and social problems of countries like France and Germany point in the direction of less central planning and regulation, not more. Perhaps the peoples of Europe, given greater freedom to make their own choices, will opt for a more perfect continental union, but this remains to be seen. Our role must be to encourage the European governments to trust their own people and to respect their decisions, at the same time we demand the same of our own government.

America's Destiny. Only the United States can inspire and guide a revival of the global revolution, because America is not a traditional nation. We are the embodiment of an idea: the sovereignty of a free people defined by a commitment to the rights and obligations embodied in the written law, rather than by a shared ancestry. Our national interests cannot be defined in purely geopolitical terms because we seek to advance ideals. Therefore, our foreign policy must be ideological, designed to advance freedom. Three times in this century we and our friends and allies have been attacked by the enemies of freedom, and three times we have prevailed, because of the incomparable power and creativity that only free people, bound together by a common purpose, can generate. In these days of multicultural relativism, it is unfashionable to state openly what the rest of the world takes for granted: the superiority of American civilization.

It is time for a Contract with the World that reasserts our willingness to resume our historic mission and recommit ourselves to support the Second Democratic Revolution. Since Clinton has proved that he cannot play this role, the signers of the contract will have to be Republicans, old-fashioned Democrats, and independents. Here is a first draft:

• *First: Our mission is the advance of freedom.* The enslavement of men and women anywhere diminishes us all. We will therefore support democracies, old and new, and we will support democrats wherever and whenever we can. The next presidency will be a platform for democratic advocacy and for the relentless denunciation of tyranny and slavery. The new secretary of state will not be a political fixer or a corporate lawyer; he or she will be someone whose career and commitment bespeak an unwavering dedication to democratic causes.

• *Second: We will revive linkage.* We will make no concessions and give no money to tyrants. We will promise the American taxpayers that their money will be spent to advance freedom, not to strengthen the slavemasters: no most-favored-nation status to a China that exploits slave labor, tortures and murders its own democrats, and intimidates democratic neighbors; no aid to Russia so long as the Yeltsin regime brazenly violates its agreements with us and marches on its neighbors; no aid to a Bulgarian regime that recollectivizes agriculture and deep-sixes the privatization program; no money to corrupt tyrants who pocket the bulk of our aid and dribble a few fragments to their people.

Having developed the most sophisticated money-tracking system in the world, we will put it to work for the new democrats, so that they will have a chance to recover at least some of the wealth stolen from them by their present and former rulers, from Russia, Bulgaria, and Romania to Mexico, Zaire, Zambia, and Tanzania. In the future, American money will fund projects, not regimes. We want to create new wealth, not redistribute our resources.

• *Third: We want to enable the citizens of the new democracies to make informed decisions about their leaders.* We will publish our files from the cold war that deal with the domestic and international activities of the Communist elites. We will call on the countries of the old empire to do the same and will make money available for the project. To those who assert that this represents improper meddling in the internal affairs of other countries, we respond that the Soviet Empire no longer exists and that in a democracy all leaders must be held accountable for their behavior, past, present, and future.

• *Fourth: While we believe in free trade, we do not believe in strengthening the enemies of freedom.* The greatest folly of the past eight years has been the dismantling of the system of international export controls that restricted the sale of advanced military technology to rogue countries. Today, countries like North Korea, China, Iraq, Iran, and Libya are buying weapons of mass destruction—and the technology to manufacture them—from the West, including the United States. We will tighten restrictions on our own military and dual-use technology exports and work with the other advanced industrial countries to recreate the system of high-tech export controls that worked so well against the Soviet Empire.

• *Fifth: We will take every legitimate step to transform tyrannies into free societies, even when this means challenging "friendly tyrants."* It is sometimes necessary to ally ourselves with antidemocratic regimes—as with the Soviet Union in World War II or with Iran and China in the cold war—but it is only a matter of time before the American people turn against such alliances. Tactical considerations can only temporarily override our strategic mission. Today, we must insist that friendly authoritarian regimes in the Middle East, Africa, and Asia share power with their own people. China may yet embrace democratic capitalism, but the gerontarchs have shown great fear of real democracy in Taiwan and Hong Kong. To have true friendship with us, the Chinese must liberalize their polity as well as their economy.

In the case of antidemocratic enemies, we will attempt to weaken and replace the oppressive regimes and will give all possible support to democratic forces seeking to defeat them. We prefer that this support be open, but it will sometimes be necessary to do it discreetly, depending on the needs of the democrats.

• *Sixth: We will restore and expand America's voice to the peoples of the world.* Radio broadcasts of the truth played a heroic role in our defeat of the Communist empire, and there are now even more ways to reach those whose governments do not want them to know the truth. We will use all means, from radio to direct satellite broadcasting and the Internet, to advance freedom in all its forms. We will not hesitate to inform the Chinese people directly that their government is violating both international standards of civilized behavior and its signed agreements with the United States, or ask the Japanese people why their government makes them pay triple the world price for rice, or tell the Iranians that we hope one day to welcome them back to the family of normal nations, or express our disgust to the peoples of Africa at the practice of chattel slavery by Mauritania and Sudan.

• *Seventh: We will provide safe haven for political refugees.* Unlike Clinton, we will not send Cuban freedom seekers back to Castro's evil island.

• *Eighth: We will build the best possible missile defense system.* We have heard Chinese military leaders threaten to send missiles into Los Angeles, and we know that the fanatics in Iran, Libya, and Iraq are building missiles to carry their new chemical and biological warheads and are racing to get nuclear weapons.

• *Ninth: We will embrace the new democracies of Central Europe and the Baltics and urge our NATO allies to expand the alliance to include them.*

• *Tenth: We do not intend to wait for the next Pearl Harbor to build a military force capable of defeating our next enemy.* The Clinton administration has permitted rogue nations to acquire advanced technology that can be used against us in the near future, and we will immediately call on the intelligence community and the Joint Chiefs of Staff to assess the implications for our own security. This done, we will take the appropriate steps to strengthen our armed forces. Serious leaders are expected to protect against worst-case scenarios.

In short, we pledge to the peoples of the world, friend and foe alike, that we will do our very best to complete the global Democratic Revolution that began more than twenty years ago with the fall of the Latin European dictatorships in Spain and Portugal, continued with the dramatic transformation of Latin

America, destroyed the Soviet Empire, gave hope to the peoples of Africa, inspired the creation of new democracies in Asia, and unleashed the creative rage of the American electorate in 1994. We do not expect to complete this great mission in the lifetime of the next administration or even in the lifetime of living Americans. The struggle against evil on this earth is eternal. But we will be faithful to our calling, secure in our democratic faith, and resolute in our pursuit of freedom for all mankind.

The failure of current Western leadership has set back the cause of the Democratic Revolution, but it may yet prove to be a blessing in disguise. The political universe in the established democracies is in turmoil, because the people know their leaders are unworthy and feel themselves ready and able to take control of their own destinies. Let us now do that and thereby ensure that our representatives do the same.

NOTES

CHAPTER 1: INTRODUCTION

1. See François Fejtö, *La Fine delle Democrazie Popolari* (Milan: Mondadori, 1994), who deals elegantly with this terrible problem: "Perhaps the most difficult problem for the countries of Central and Eastern Europe at the end of communism—more difficult than the reform of the institutions or the passage to a market economy—was the change of model of behavior, of way of life, of mentality" (p. 394).

CHAPTER 2: ORIGINS OF THE REVOLUTION

1. R. R. Palmer, *The Age of the Democratic Revolution,* vol. 1 (Princeton: Princeton University Press, 1959), pp. 189–90.

2. *Ibid.,* p. 214.

3. *Ibid.,* p. 215.

4. Louis Hartz, *The Liberal Tradition* (New York: Harcourt Brace, 1955).

5. The intrinsically paradoxical nature of American civilization is wonderfully discussed in Michael Kamen, *People of Paradox* (New York: Random House, 1972).

6. See Jacques Godechot's classic, *The Counter Revolution* (New York: Howard Fertig, 1971).

7. See Jacob L. Talmon, *The Origins of Totalitarian Democracy* (London: Secker's Warburg, 1952).

8. Demands for greater executive power were made later on, when legislatures were stalemated over specific reform programs, but this is a different question.

9. Discussing the 1976 publication of Varlam Salamov's great work *Stories of the Kolyma,* the director of the Savelli publishing house in Italy

recalled "a near total silence, and the book was one of our most notable failures." And a journalist writing about the episode in *La Stampa* (November 20, 1992) wryly noted that "23 years after the death of Stalin, the Gulag was still taboo."

10. The best book on the subject is Shirley Christian, *Nicaragua: Revolution in the Family* (New York: Random House, 1985).

11. King Juan Carlos and President Suarez actually designed and executed a strategy for the peaceful transition from dictatorship to democracy, thereby providing a model for the entire world. No one more than they deserved the Nobel Peace Prize, but it was not offered to them. Instead, it was given to Gorbachev, who neither wanted nor achieved a transition to democracy. Yet such is the prestige of the Nobel Prize that most people think of Gorbachev as the great revolutionary, and very few are aware of the far more important actions of Juan Carlos and Suarez.

12. The phrase comes from a CIA biography of Cunhal written in the early 1970s.

13. One of the interesting themes in the Portuguese stories is the behavior of Brandt, who advocated a soft line—some would say appeasement—toward the Soviet Union on most major issues. Yet in the Portuguese case, Brandt poured assistance to Soares and the Socialists and organized every kind of support from other members of the Socialist International. Later, he and Soares, who was much tougher on the Soviets, would often disagree on East-West issues in debates within the European bureau of the International.

14. There was one lunatic outburst of violence after the transition had been achieved, when a member of the Guardia Civil opened fire in Parliament and announced he was leading a coup. But it only lasted one night and gave the king an opportunity to go on national television and assure the country that Spain was not about to fall back into dictatorship.

15. Of course, many Western leaders took seriously Ceausescu's claim to be an "independent" leader, so the knowledge of the Carrillo-Ceausescu relationship might not have worked against the Spaniard.

16. I had a fascinating conversation with De Klerk just a few weeks before Mandela's release, and he spent close to an hour discussing Spain. It was clear from the discussion that he was about to release Mandela and that Juan Carlos's handling of Carrillo was a model for him.

17. I believe the phrase was first used by Norman Podhoretz, the editor of *Commentary*. For a brilliant discussion of the power of this pernicious idea, see Francois Furet, *La fin d'une illusion* (Paris: Flammarion, 1995).

18. See Michael A. Ledeen, "Renzo de Felice and the Controversy over Italian Fascism," in George L. Mosse, ed., *International Fascism: New Thoughts and New Approaches* (New York: Sage, 1979). Sadly, there was a replay of the assault against De Felice in the winter of 1992, when leftist extremists demonstrated at the opening of the academic year at Rome Uni-

versity, accusing De Felice of being a fascist apologist.

19.   See Michael A. Ledeen, "Raymond Aron: The Outsider as Out-sider," in *Society,* vol. 21, no. 4 (1984), reprinted in *Proceedings of the American Philosophical Society,* vol. 138, no. 1 (1994).

20.   Raymond Aron, *In Defense of Decadent Europe* (South Bend, Ind.: Regnery Gateway, 1977), p. 27.

21.   Texts of speeches by Sandinista leaders in closed-session meetings with party cadres were obtained by the U.S. government and published by the Department of State.

22.   The document is reproduced in Vladimir Bukovsky, *Jugement à Moscou* (Paris: Robert Laffont, 1995), p. 41.

23.   Handal's letter and the Soviet Central Committee documents approving the requests are reproduced. Ibid., p. 39.

CHAPTER 3: HIGH TIDE OF THE REVOLUTION

1.   Martin Malia, "The Yeltsin Revolution," *New Republic,* February 10, 1992.

2.   See Michael A. Ledeen, "A Mensch in the Vatican," in *The American Zionist* (June–July 1979).

3.   Quoted in David Willey, *Il politico di Dio* (Milan: Longanesi, 1992), p. 142.

4.   Ibid.

5.   George Weigel, *The Final Revolution* (New York: Oxford University Press, 1992), p. 102.

6.   If one needed any additional confirmation of the pope's worldview, it was made luminously clear in his choice of personal secretaries. There were two of them, a Pole named Dziwisz and a Zairean, Everett Kabongo. Both were intellectually brilliant, personally intense, and tireless workers. In my regular meetings with Kabongo over a period of several years, I found him the toughest person—intellectually, that is—I had ever worked with. Although he cannot be much more than five-feet six or seven inches tall, he is the sort who could play middle linebacker for the Bears, admittedly an odd image for a man of the cloth who served for several years as personal secretary to Pope John Paul II, and who, throughout dozens of hours of conversation about subjects ranging from the Judaism of the Blessed Virgin to the shortcomings of the U.S. government, never raised his voice, and always conveyed criticism in a tone of sadness, never in anger or sarcasm.

Notwithstanding the gentle comportment one would expect from an eminent *monsignore,* he is blessed with an uncompromisingly rigorous intellect and a Zen-like disciplined patience. Perhaps because of his African upbringing—his father was the chief of one of the largest tribes in Zaire—he seemed always to have an unhurried, even serene air. I always looked forward to working my way through the labyrinths of the Vatican to a small antechamber just off the "Throne Room" where John Paul received official visitors. The contrast could hardly have been more dramatic: the Throne Room was enormous, with heavy gold decorations surrounding the Renaissance and baroque paintings and frescoes. The antechamber was small and austere, with a simple crucifix on one wall and a modernistic Madonna in a plain wooden frame on the wall opposite, and one small, rectangular wooden table with two facing straightbacked wooden chairs. There we would sit and talk as long as four hours, with never an interruption. Not a telephone ring, not a rap at the door, not even a passing footfall. The tranquillity of the setting undoubtedly encourages the men of the Vatican to think in long periods of time, just as the rushed, high-pressure atmosphere in Western foreign ministries and presidencies compresses their thinking to short terms.

The sort of philosophical, wide-ranging discussion that Kabongo favored could not possibly take place in the office of any top official of any first-world government. All those countries are too closely tied to the clock—to busy daily schedules and deadlines and press conferences and sound bites and election campaigns—to permit them the kind of quiet contemplation and thoughtful exchange of ideas that constitute so much of the work of the Holy See.

7.   Marvin Kalb was later to confirm the existence of this message, and he announced it on his televised investigation for NBC News into the papal assassination attempt.

8.   I wrote in *Grave New World* (New York: Oxford University Press, 1985) that the entire empire was at stake in the Soviets' quest for some sort of solution to the crisis of legitimacy raised by Solidarity. At the time the overwhelming majority of "experts" and policy analysts believed that the movement had been crushed. The few who saw how grave the crisis really was—especially in light of what we knew about the economic strains on the empire—were highly independent people like Richard Perle, William Casey, Stephen Bryen, and Herb Meyer.

9.   There seems to be little doubt, for example, that the Vatican channeled funds to democratic resistance groups in both South America and the Soviet Empire. Some of the money seems to have passed through the Ambrosiano Bank.

10.   *Le Monde*, November 17, 1990. Quoted in Fejtö, *La Fine delle Democrazie Popolari* (Milan: Mondadori, 1994), p. 199.

11.   Anthony C. Sutton, *Western Technology and Soviet Economic Development*, in three vols. (Palo Alto: Hoover Institution Press, 1968–1973).

12.   Vladimir Bukovsky, *To Choose Freedom* (Palo Alto: Stanford University Press, 1987), p. 146.

13.   This, at least, is the version that reached the West from, among other sources, the controversial "defector" Yurchenko. It is a wonderful

story, but it may have been concocted to protect the real source of KGB information about Farewell, which might have been somebody like their CIA agent, Aldrich Ames.

14.   It is symptomatic of the confused state of the professoriat that Paul Kennedy's thesis—claiming that the United States was guilty of "imperial overreach," while the Soviet Empire was much more stable—gained such popularity, just as the Soviet Empire was about to crash and burn.

15.   Indeed, until the early 1980s, the CIA had East Germany at least even with West Germany, and in some respects more advanced.

16.   Polish General Jan Sejna, who defected to the United States in 1968, has testified that Warsaw Pact leaders were informed at the highest level that the Soviet Union intended to lure the West into a false sense of security and obtain Western credits and technology through a strategic deception pretending that the Kremlin was liberalizing at home and ending the hostility between the two blocs internationally.

17.   Tatyana Tolstaya, "When Putsch Comes to Shove," *New Republic,* September 16 and 23, 1991.

18.   Mikhail Heller, *Cogs in the Wheel: The Formation of Soviet Man* (New York: Knopf, 1988), p. xvii.

19.   *New York Times,* January 26, 1995.

20.   David E. Apter, "Institutionalism Reconsidered," *International Social Science Journal* (August 1991).

21.   Heller, *Cogs in the Wheel,* pp. 262–63.

22.   The notes for several of these meetings were passed on to me by Irving Brown of the AFL-CIO.

23.   William H. Luers, "Czechoslovakia: The Road to Revolution," *Foreign Affairs* (Spring 1990), p. 88.

24.   Ibid., p. 90.

25.   Ibid., p. 98.

26.   Willey, *Il politico di Dio,* p. 74.

CHAPTER 4: THE REVOLUTION BETRAYED

1.   We were not alone in appeasing Gorbachev at the expense of the democrats; British Foreign Secretary Douglas Hurd muttered on national television that the Lithuanians were "not . . . really worthy of diplomatic consideration." See Leopold Labedz, "Moment of Truth," *Encounter* (July-August 1990), p. 14.

2.   Bukovsky, armed with a computer and a scanner thanks to the advice and assistance of Stephen Bryen—one of the two persons sent by AEI to Moscow in early 1992—stumbled onto a treasure trove of three thousand pages of documents. These were summoned by the Russian government in connection with the hearing, before the Constitutional Court, of the old

Communist Party's challenge to Yeltsin's banning of the party.

3.   Yevgeniya Albats, "KGB-MSB-MVBD: Substantive Changes?" *Moscow News,* no. 2, January 13, 1992, p. 5. Quoted in J. Michael Waller, *Commonwealth of Czekists: The Former KGB Is Alive and Well in Post-Soviet Society,* in John W. Blaney, ed., *The Successor States to the USSR* (Washington, D.C.: Congressional Quarterly, 1995), p. 50.

4.   This is not to say that there were no "defections in place"; there may have been some. Western intelligence services would certainly have liked to keep high-level spies in Russia and other former bloc countries.

5.   Richard Perle, "Warren Christopher, Call Your Office," *International Economy* (July–August 1995).

CHAPTER 5: THE STRUGGLE FOR UNDERSTANDING

1.   François Furet, *Il Passato di un'Illusione* (Milan: Mondalori, 1995), p. 24.

2.   The responses to his article were published before he even had a chance to read them, let alone reply.

3.   Jean-François Revel, *La Connaissance Inutile* (New York: Random House, 1991), pp. 373–74.

4.   See Michael A. Ledeen, *Grave New World* (New York: Oxford University Press, 1985), p. 103ff.

5.   Quoted in Robert Conquest, *Present Danger* (Stanford, Calif.: Hoover Institution Press, 1979), pp. 129–30.

6.   Yuri B. Shvets, *Washington Station* (New York: Simon and Schuster, 1994).

7.   In 1996, when two of its journalists won Pulitzer Prizes, the *New York Times* proudly published a long list of previous winners, including the infamous Walter Duranty, who wrote puff pieces about the Soviet Union while in the employ of the Soviet intelligence services. One would hope that the *Times* would be sufficiently embarrassed by this scandal to remove Duranty from the list, or at least to acknowledge that he was working for our enemies, but nothing of the sort has taken place.

8.   Carl N. Degler, *Out of Our Past* (New York: Harper, 1959), pp. 270–73.

9.   Perhaps the worst moment came at Stanford University, where Bukovsky was studying in the early 1980s. The university decided to give an award to a group of Soviet "doctors," including those who had consigned Bukovsky to the "mental hospitals" where he was subjected to torture using psychotropic drugs. When he protested to the university authorities, he was dismissed out of hand.

10.   Robert W. Fogel, "The Fourth Great Awakening and the Political Realignment of the 1990s," presented at the American Enterprise Institute,

April 27, 1995.

11.   Ibid.

12.   Walter Dean Burnham, "The Fourth American Republic?" *Wall Street Journal,* October 16, 1995.

13.   The worldwide explosion of radical Islam is similarly a revolt against the corruption of the traditional elites, although it is certainly not friendly to the Democratic Revolution.

CHAPTER 6: THE FUTURE OF THE REVOLUTION

1.   Phillip Dimitrov, *New York Times,* March 23, 1992.

2.   Anne Applebaum, "The Fall and Rise of the Communists," *Foreign Affairs* (November–December 1994).

3.   Ian Mihai Pacepa, "Moscow's Dnestr Plan in Action," unpublished essay (1994).

4.   It seems that Western intelligence organizations, which should certainly have been tracking gold sales (both as an indicator of the gravity of the Soviet crisis and as a warning sign of international monetary problems) failed to notice that the entire reserves of the Soviet Union had been sold off. Happily, there were no damaging consequences to the West as a result of the Soviet collapse, for if there had been, the intelligence services would have been responsible for the greatest intelligence failure since Pearl Harbor.

5.   The best study is Claire Sterling, *Thieves' World* (New York: Simon and Schuster, 1994).

6.   Michael Radu, "Life after Death," *Society* (January–February 1993).

7.   Augusto Segre, *Mose* (Rome: Editrice Esperienze, 1975), p. 296.

8.   See the outstanding collection of essays on "Democracy in Taiwan," in *World Affairs* (Fall 1992 and Winter 1993), edited by Chong-Pin Lin.

9.   Mario Vargas Llosa, *The News,* Mexico City, November 9, 1993.

10.   This is not to say that the bureaucrats themselves do not have a fairly clear political profile; American liberals enjoy and endorse bureaucracy more than conservatives do (in Western Europe, most conservatives are nearly as statist as the Left). In the degenerate version of contemporary liberalism, the liberals scorn innovation, eccentricity, and enterprise; they prefer to legislate, regulate, and enforce. Bureaucracy is the weapon of choice for those who distrust the people; those who prefer the freedom to make their own mistakes hate the bureaucracy.

11.   Juan Linz and Alfred Stepan, "The Exit from Communism," *Daedalus* (Spring 1992), p. 124.

INDEX

143

Contract with the World, American, 147–79

Contra movement, 30–32

Coordinating Committee for Multilateral Export Contols. *See* COCOM

Corruption: in Communist dictatorships, 131; in Italy, 123–25; in Russia, 133–34; in West, 122

Craxi, Bettino, 124

Croatians, 84

Cuba, 23, 29, 51–52, 87

Cult of the state, 1

Cultural Revolution (China), 94

Cultural shift, from intellectual to popular, 117–18

Cunhal, Alvaro, 17, 19

Czechoslovakia, 4, 57, 58, 129, 132

Czech Republic, 72; no resurgence of Communists, 131–33

Deaver, Michael, 32, 47

De Felice, Renzo, 25–26, 114

Degler, Carl N., 112, 158n8

de Klerk, F. W., 24, 154n16

De Michelis, Gianni, 124

Democracy and wealth, causal relationship, 140

Democratic capitalism, 92, 117, 118, 120, 127; and intellectuals, 94–95; in Italy, 127

Democratic Party (U.S.), 4, 122

Democratic Revolution, 1–2, 7, 28, 120; American Revolution fullest example, 9; and changes in Western welfare states, 75; definition, 3; difficulties of new democracies.127–30, 135–36, 145–46; failure of Americans to live up to its ideals, 113–14; failure to put Communists on trial, 68, 70; global purge, 121–22; Iberian model of, 15–22; leaders of, 120; and less government, 88–89; and myths of

cold war era, 22; need for military power, 144; and 1994 U.S. elections, 88–90; no aid from United States, 63–64; origins of, 11–15; paradoxical, 11; and pope, 40–41; in Portugal, 17–20; and religion, 118–19; roadblocks to, 91–94; in South Africa, 140; in Spain, 15–17

D'Encausse, Hélène Carrére, 28, 51

Deng Xiaoping, 94

Desert Shame, 66, 72

Desert Storm, 65, 66

de Tocqueville, Alexis, 120

Dimitrov, Phillip, 128, 130, 159n1

Dissidents in Soviet bloc, 57–58

Duarte, José Napoleon, 30, 31

Duranty, Walter, 158n7

Eanes, Ramalho, 17

East Germany, 34, 48, 57, 69, 132

Elections of 1994 (U.S.), 87–90

El Salvador, 29, 30–32

Embargoes, 86–87

Ethnos, Soviet-backed newspaper in Greece, 100–104

European Union, 146

Evangelical Christianity, 119

Exodus, parallel to post–Soviet Union countries, 136–37

Export controls, 46, 77, 83

Farewell (espionage), 44–46

Fascism: and communism compared by De Felice, 25–26; in Italy, 25–26; revival, 130

Fejtö, François, 153n1, 156n10

First Democratic Revolution, 141

Fogel, Robert W., 118, 158nn10, 11

Forbes, Malcolm, 95

Ford, Gerald, 66

France: collapse of Communist ideology in, 27; history of bureaucracy in, 141–42; and technological espionage in Russia, 45–46

ABOUT THE AUTHOR

MICHAEL A. LEDEEN, who holds the Freedom Chair at the American Enterprise Institute in Washington, D.C., is an authority on intelligence and international affairs.

Formerly the Rome correspondent for the *New Republic* and the founding editor of the *Washington Quarterly*, Ledeen is currently foreign editor of the *American Spectator*, a contributor to the *Wall Street Journal*, the *Weekly Standard*, and *National Review*, an adviser to multinational corporations in Europe, Africa, and the United States, and a corporate director in American and African organizations.

He has been profiled in the *New York Times* and was the subject of a front-page article and a lead editorial in the *Wall Street Journal*. A profile of him concluded that "a portrait emerges of a man with an intense knowledge of 20th-century history, a deep commitment to democracy, and a willingness to be adventurous. This is a man who has helped shape American foreign policy at its highest levels." As Ted Koppel puts it, "Michael Ledeen is a Renaissance man . . . in the tradition of Machiavelli."

He is also a celebrated scholar and lecturer. He holds a Ph.D. in history and philosophy from the University of Wisconsin and has been the recipient of many awards and research grants. His eleven books include *Grave New World*, which predicted the crisis of the Soviet Empire five years before it occurred, and *Perilous Statecraft*, recently praised as the most accurate account of the Iran-contra affair. His essays in *Commentary*, the *New Republic*, and the *American Spectator* have been reprinted in dozens of languages around the world.

167

William M. Landes
Clifton R. Musser Professor of
  Economics
University of Chicago Law School

Sam Peltzman
Sears Roebuck Professor of Economics
  and Financial Services
University of Chicago
  Graduate School of Business

Nelson W. Polsby
Professor of Political Science
University of California at Berkeley

George L. Priest
John M. Olin Professor of Law and
  Economics
Yale Law School

Murray L. Weidenbaum
Mallinckrodt Distinguished
  University Professor
Washington University

Research Staff

Leon Aron
Resident Scholar

Claude E. Barfield
Resident Scholar; Director, Science
  and Technology Policy Studies

Cynthia A. Beltz
Research Fellow

Walter Berns
Resident Scholar

Douglas J. Besharov
Resident Scholar

Robert H. Bork
John M. Olin Scholar in Legal Studies

Karlyn Bowman
Resident Fellow

John E. Calfee
Resident Scholar

Lynne V. Cheney
W. H. Brady, Jr., Distinguished Fellow

Stephen R. Conafay
Executive Fellow

Dinesh D'Souza
John M. Olin Research Fellow

Nicholas N. Eberstadt
Visiting Scholar

Mark Falcoff
Resident Scholar

John D. Fonte
Visiting Scholar

Gerald R. Ford
Distinguished Fellow

Murray F. Foss
Visiting Scholar

Diana Furchtgott-Roth
Assistant to the President and Resident
  Fellow

Suzanne Garment
Resident Scholar

Jeffrey Gedmin
Research Fellow

Patrick Glynn
Resident Scholar

Robert A. Goldwin
Resident Scholar

Robert W. Hahn
Resident Scholar

Thomas Hazlett
Visiting Scholar

Robert B. Helms
Resident Scholar; Director, Health
  Policy Studies

Glenn Hubbard
Visiting Scholar

Douglas Irwin
Henry Wendt Scholar in Political
  Economy

James D. Johnston
Resident Fellow

Jeane J. Kirkpatrick
Senior Fellow; Director, Foreign and
  Defense Policy Studies

Marvin H. Kosters
Resident Scholar; Director,
  Economic Policy Studies

Irving Kristol
John M. Olin Distinguished Fellow

Dana Lane
Director of Publications

Michael A. Ledeen
Resident Scholar

James Lilley
Resident Fellow; Director, Asian
  Studies Program

John H. Makin
Resident Scholar; Director, Fiscal
  Policy Studies

Allan H. Meltzer
Visiting Scholar

Joshua Muravchik
Resident Scholar

Charles Murray
Bradley Fellow

Michael Novak
George F. Jewett Scholar in Religion,
  Philosophy, and Public Policy;
  Director, Social and
  Political Studies

Norman J. Ornstein
Resident Scholar

Richard N. Perle
Resident Fellow

William Schneider
Resident Scholar

William Shew
Visiting Scholar

J. Gregory Sidak
F. K. Weyerhaeuser Fellow

Herbert Stein
Senior Fellow

Irwin M. Stelzer
Resident Scholar; Director, Regulatory
  Policy Studies

W. Allen Wallis
Resident Scholar

Ben J. Wattenberg
Senior Fellow

Carolyn L. Weaver
Resident Scholar; Director, Social
  Security and Pension Studies

A NOTE ON THE BOOK

*This book was edited by Dana Lane
of the publications staff
of the American Enterprise Institute.
The index was prepared by Nancy Rosenberg.
The text was set in Sabon.
Lisa Roman and Jennifer Lesiak
of the AEI Press set the type,
and Edwards Brothers, Incorporated,
of Lillington, North Carolina,
printed and bound the book,
using permanent acid-free paper.*

The AEI Press is the publisher for the American Enterprise Institute for Public Policy Research, 1150 Seventeenth Street, N.W., Washington, D.C. 20036; *Christopher C. DeMuth,* publisher; *Dana Lane,* director; *Ann Petty,* editor; *Leigh Tripoli,* editor; *Cheryl Weissman,* editor; *Jennifer Lesiak,* editorial assistant.